Tea Party Talk: The Governors

Amy Fried and Jim Melcher

To my wonderful children, Sarah and Caleb

Amy Fried

To my biggest heroes -- my parents John W. and Beatrice Melcher, who have shared many cups of tea in their 66 years of marriage.

Jim Melcher

CONTENTS

ACKNOWLEDGMENTS

Many people have had a hand in moving this book forward and we want to thank as many of them as we can think of. The original inspiration came from Sandy Caron. We'd like to thank the students who helped us with organization and with quotation and information gathering: Isaac Frith, Meghan Williams, Liam Nee, and Alexandria Jesiolowski. Our Facebook friends offered suggestions on potential titles. George Danby, the book's cover art designer, did a wonderful job and was a pleasure to work with, as was graphic artist Mary Ann Parks. Our colleagues at our respective colleges offered encouragement. We also received useful feedback from the panel and audience at the New England Political Science Association Convention in the spring of 2012, where we presented a scholarly paper on the rhetoric of Tea Party governors. Peter Melcher offered technical advice. Our spouses were, as always, sources of support in so many ways.

And, finally, we want to acknowledge the Tea Party governors themselves. Without them, there couldn't have been this book at all!

INTRODUCTION

It wasn't long ago a new political movement seemed to spring up out of nowhere, with gatherings of activists holding pamphlet-sized copies of the Constitution and attendees wearing tri-cornered hats, waist-coats and knee-breeches. Carrying grassroots energy and aided by nationally funded, centrally organized groups, the Tea Party influenced some Republican primaries, driving out established, respected incumbents who were seen as too willing to compromise. In 2010, some Tea Party candidates were too far to the right for their states and districts and lost. A good many won.

Tea Party talk was strong and sharp. Tea Party politicians were direct about what they wanted government to do - and not do. And, as political scientists and political junkies, we listened.

One place where Tea Party candidates won big was in the states. In 2010, 18 legislatures and 11 governorships flipped from Democratic to Republican. We live in Maine, a state that changed completely, from a Democrat in the Governor's mansion and Democratic-controlled legislature to Republicans holding both for the first time since the mid-1960s. Our own governor, Paul LePage, is included in this book and his words gave us the inspiration for the illustration on our front cover by George Danby, editorial cartoonist for the Bangor Daily News. When asked about moving an eagle's nest near a proposed highway bypass, LePage said, "I absolutely believe the federal government should put people ahead of eagles. We've gotten to a point in our society where people don't count. People pay taxes, eagles don't." [1]

This book includes quotations from LePage and thirteen other Tea Party governors, said when they campaigned and when they governed, with everything from formal statements in proclamations and speeches to off-the-cuff comments to crowds and reporters to Facebook posts (South Carolina's Nikki Haley is especially well-known for her Facebook observations).

Our group of Tea Party governors, all Republicans, is not necessarily exhaustive. But all of the governors we selected were identified in the mass media as reflecting Tea Party themes, were the beneficiaries of Tea Party support, or proclaimed themselves to be Tea Party backers.

When in doubt, we stayed as close to the source as possible: we first relied on what the governors themselves said about the Tea Party movement, and we placed more emphasis on what people said about these governors in their own states than what the national media has said. For example, Louisiana Governor Bobby Jindal has sometimes been described as a Tea Party governor in the national press. In his home state, however, Tea Party activists and bloggers have complained loudly that he hasn't been fiscally conservative enough and that he has seldom been seen at Tea Party-affiliated events. As a result, we didn't include him in this book.

Although we are political scientists, this is not a work of social science. It doesn't use statistics and we don't claim to have a random sample of these governors' utterances. (And, you sure don't need a degree in political science to enjoy it!) Instead, we attempt to hold up a net and capture the governors' sensibilities to show what they talk about and care about.

In one way, though, we did act like political scientists: We tried to be fair and as objective as possible in choosing which quotations to use. Of course, we leaned toward picking colorful quotes, like the one we borrowed for our book title. But we wanted the readers of this book to get a feel for the priorities of what these men and women stand for. We want, in short, to let the Tea Party governors speak for themselves. We come neither to exalt nor to tear them down, but to show their perspectives in their words. (And, hopefully, we've done a good enough job of it that you'll enjoy the book no matter what your stand is on the Tea Party.)

As you read through the quotations, you'll have your own reactions. We came to three broad conclusions.

1. The job of governor pushes these elected officials to, well, govern.

Indeed, a funny thing happened when it came time for governing. Protesting and campaigning allow people to say all sorts of things that may not work out well in practice.

And nowhere else does the most practical matter than in the governor's office. In the U.S. House and Senate, legislators can stand up for principles without budging, even refusing to raise the debt limit, a step needed to pay bills already incurred.

State governors are obligated to get it done. Budgets must be passed -- and balanced. Schools have to be funded. Debts have to be serviced. State prisons have to operate. At the same time, governors can't just do what they want. So many programs operate with at least some federal funds, bringing many controls and limits on state action. And the state legislature, courts, and people will have their own say.

As Republicans took a majority of seats in the U.S. House of Representatives and made gains in the Senate, newly elected Republican, Tea Party-leaning governors moved quickly. In January 2011, "In Washington, the GOP-led House delivered symbolism at first . . . It would take weeks to get GOP troops lined up to start fighting consequential budget wars with the Democrats. Quicker off the mark were Tea Party-aligned governors backed by large legislative majorities." [1] Tea Party governors cut taxes, with most gains going to upper-income earners and businesses, while saying that revenue shortfalls required cutting spending on health care, education, and public employees' pensions: "GOPers in the states also moved quickly to ram through legislative blueprints disseminated by conservative think tanks - to curb the power of employee unions, eliminate business regulations, and toughen up rules affecting how citizens register to vote or actually vote on election day." [2] Many adopted model-legislation from ALEC, the American Legislative Exchange Council.

2. Tea Party style.

Some tea party governors are brash, even outrageous. However, while these Tea Party governors agree a lot on taxes and spending and other policies, they are not identical in style and temperament.

After taking office, some Tea Party governors continued to use sharp language, sometimes pushing back hard at political opponents, ordinary citizens and the press. In Maine, Governor Paul LePage gained a reputation for intemperate remarks and for stirring up symbolic controversies, like removing a mural celebrating labor history. Governor Kasich of Ohio and Governor Christie of New Jersey were sometimes belligerent.

Many Tea Party governors are quite effective, whether in spite of or because of tough rhetoric. Tough, even mean talk can rally one's support, but that kind of talk can push independents away and may even undermine the governor's relationship with legislators from his or her party. For instance, Governor LePage met with members of his party caucus about, he said, "zipping my mouth up and not offending them" and received a letter from eight state Senate Republicans who urged him to abandon "government by disrespect." [3] Later some Republican legislators criticized him for calling state workers "corrupt" and saying the Internal Revenue Service is the "new Gestapo." [4]

As we've said, not all of these governors had a bellicose style. And even the most sharp-tongued Tea Party governors often spoke with calm and civility, clearly expressing their views on what policies they want and what they desire for their states. But the brash statements played a big part in media coverage and in shaping some governors' images.

3. While Tea Party governors and movement activists agree about a lot, they don't necessarily talk about the same issues.

For instance, despite activists' statements about the founders (and occasional Revolutionary-era dress), most Tea Party governors had little to say about the framers of the Constitution. (Rick Perry would probably be the leading exception.)

In fact, Tea Party governors mostly talk about policy issues and their policy opponents. Their policy views are quite conservative, with a strong emphasis on promoting business interests and, to a lesser degree, limits on abortion, gay rights, and contraception. Moreover, while some Tea Party governors reject compromise, others do not. Yet, given their stalwart anti-tax, socially conservative and anti-economic regulation views, some of these governors, in essence, were "Tea Party" before there was a Tea Party.

Where did the Tea Party come from?

On January 20, 2009, Barack Obama was sworn into office as the 44th President of the United States. Obama won 53% of the vote and a two-to-one margin in the Electoral College. Amidst great hopes and with attention to his historic status as the first African-American to attain the presidency, Obama's inauguration drew a huge audience to the National Mall and to broadcast and internet outlets. President Obama came into office as the economy was plunging further into recession, with economic conditions that included a financial and housing crisis.

Less than a month after Obama was sworn in, the Tea Party began. Most observers date its start to February 19, 2009 when CNBC's Rick Santelli spoke out against the president's plan to block foreclosures. In the "Santelli rant," the broadcaster said:

The government is promoting bad behavior . . . Why don't you put up a website to have people vote on the internet as a referendum to see if we really want to subsidize the losers' mortgages? Or would they like to at least buy cars, buy a house that is in foreclosure … give it to people who might have a chance to actually prosper down the road and reward people that can carry the water instead of drink the water? This is America! (He turns to the traders nearby) How many people want to pay for your neighbor's mortgages that has an extra bathroom and can't pay their bills? Raise their hand! President Obama, are you listening? . . . It's time for another Tea Party. What we are doing in this country will make Thomas Jefferson and Benjamin Franklin roll over in their graves [5].

Santelli then called for "a Chicago Tea Party in July." The next day fifty conservative activists held a conference call to plan "coordinated protests" the following week [6]. Demonstrations reached their high point during the debates and votes surrounding the Affordable Care Act (Obamacare).

A movement both based in citizen views and organized from above, the Tea Party grew along with greater polarization in American politics, a sharp decrease in the numbers of moderate Republicans, and the rise of anti-tax, nationally-organized, corporate-funded groups. [7] Those trends took decades to unfold and set the stage (or perhaps the table) for the rise of the Tea Party.

Tea Party activists talk a lot about the founding and the Constitution and claimed today's Americans are deprived of what the founders sought - freedom, rights, and an exceedingly limited national government when it comes to the economy and regulations. However, some do call for a strong government presence in reinforcing what they see as traditional moral values-though some research suggests that this is much more true of older Tea Party activists than younger ones. Whether speaking about the bailouts of the financial sector and the automobile industry, the Affordable Care Act or housing foreclosures, supporters of the Tea Party don't just say these were ineffective policies - they say these undermine the foundations of the American system.

For many, disliking government programs is connected to the idea that giving assistance helps the undeserving, is unfair to other Americans and undermines the work ethic. As conservative populists, activists see a division between the people and elites, who, at best, are corrupt and benefit from connections and "crony capitalism." Conspiracy-oriented populists perceive hidden manipulators, linking everyone from financier George Soros to Woodrow Wilson and a myriad of organizations, activists, and political officials. In general, they believe government is too big and too powerful, with the federal government having too much control over the states.

Tea Party Governors Speak

Brought to power by the Republican sweep of 2010, with its Tea Party activism, Tea Party governors sometimes focus on very different issues than Tea Party activists.

Both talk about the legacy of American traditions, but the governors more often talk about religious traditions rather than the Founding Fathers.

South Carolina Governor Nikki Haley could hardly have been more personal: "My faith in Christ has a profound impact on my daily life and I look to Him for guidance with every decision I make. God has blessed my family in so many ways and my faith in the Lord gives me great strength on a daily basis. Being a Christian is not about words, but about living for

5

Christ every day." Sam Brownback prayed publicly in the name of Jesus, Scott Walker spoke at length with Pat Robertson's CBN about how the Christian faith of both he and his wife have helped them get through their challenges, and Rick Perry, before his appearance at "The Response," a large prayer rally at Reliant Stadium in Houston, recorded a video in which he stated "I'm all too aware of government's limitations when it comes to fixing things that are spiritual in nature. That's where prayer comes in. We need it more than ever with the economy in trouble, communities in crisis, people adrift in a sea of moral relativism. We need God's help and that's why I'm calling on Americans to pray and fast like Jesus did."

They strongly oppose abortion and a majority of these governors have signed new legislation to place greater restrictions, several of which were to bar most or all abortions after 20 weeks of pregnancy.

Tea Party governors' discussions of public policies are more practical than theoretical and, except for health care, rarely reference constitutional questions. Texas Governor Rick Perry's flirtation with Texas secession stands out even among this group. Instead, Tea Party governors emphasize the need to support business interests and to reduce welfare (a category sometimes drawn rather broadly) and to limit funds flowing to immigrants and public employees. All praise business and talk about becoming more "business-friendly;" all but one said in so many words that their state was "Open for Business." Idaho Governor Butch Otter wrote a "love letter" to businesses in neighboring states encouraging them to move there. Many draw on their personal stories to extol self-reliance and hard work.

Tea Party governors cast themselves as the ally of ordinary working people against their foes, but with a specific foe in mind: labor unions, and in particular public sector unions, such as public teacher unions (or, sometimes, public workers more generally). Often the governors say their main beef is with labor union leaders.

Some governors tout their business experience and denigrate the public sector, saying government is too expensive and too unresponsive. They often argue that high taxes harm the private sector, which they see as the heroes of job growth and prosperity. Pennsylvania Governor Tom Corbett argued, "We will not raise taxes. There is no talking around these limits. Every dollar taken in tax is one less in the hands of a job holder or job creator."

Backers of blunt Tea Party backed politicians such as Sarah Palin, Paul LePage, Chris Christie and Rick Santorum cite their candor as refreshing. [8] Republican campaign leaders like Lance Dutson, the communications director of the Republican coordinated campaign in Maine in 2010, offered, "I think people want someone that's sincere . . . I think that even beyond right or left or conservative or liberal right now, people are looking for sincerity in the people that lead them. And I think that that's something that

6

Paul [LePage] has very clearly showed and I think that's part of what's going on here." [9]

Governor John Kasich of Ohio claimed that "California . . . is filled with whackadoodles" and offered this threat to lobbyists shortly after being elected: "We need you on the bus, and if you're not on the bus, we will run over you with the bus. And I'm not kidding." Idaho Governor Butch Otter, noting California's problems, said that "if California were my horse, I would shoot it." Rick Perry said of Federal Reserve Board Chairman Ben Bernanke: "If this guy prints more money between now and the election, I don't know what y'all would do to him in Iowa, but we...would treat him pretty ugly down in Texas. Printing more money to play politics at this particular time in American history is almost treacherous or treasonous in my opinion." Chris Christie called political opponents "numb nuts" and Paul LePage said that a meeting requested by unemployed workers was "bullshit" (and repeated it more slowly for emphasis!)

Just as many Tea Party conservatives are critical of past Republican leaders for being insufficiently conservative, some Tea Party governors have cast themselves as true Republicans and conservatives. Sam Brownback questioned the conservatism of his Republican predecessors when he said "I'm the first conservative governor in probably 50 years in Kansas." Nikki Haley criticized her Republican Party establishment as insufficiently conservative when she won the 2010 gubernatorial primary: "We knew from the beginning it was us versus the establishment. We were settling (in South Carolina) for a Republican House, a Republican Senate, a Republican governor. I won't stop until we get a conservative House, a conservative Senate, a conservative governor."

Whether these governors got their wishes is hard to say, but they have certainly left a mark, and people have very strong feelings about them. Perhaps these political figures fire you up, or maybe they leave you cold. So, we invite you to sit down with a hot cup of strong tea, or perhaps a cold glass of iced tea, and read these selections from America's Tea Party governors.

"OPEN FOR BUSINESS'

Alaska, Governor Sean Parnell: "I want to send the message that Alaska is open for business and to change the attitude or perception among these companies that we are not."

Arizona, Governor Jan Brewer: "A jubilant Gov. Jan Brewer praised the Legislature's quick passage of the Arizona Competitiveness Package this week, saying it means that 'Arizona is open for business.'"

Florida, Governor Rick Scott: "Florida is open for business . . . There were plenty of pundits and insiders who said this victory was impossible, but the people of Florida knew exactly what they wanted."

Idaho, Governor C. L. "Butch" Otter: "Love Letter to Our Neighbors: Idaho Is Open For Your Business"

Kansas, Governor Sam Brownback: "We overhauled our state's economic-development system, enacted modest tax relief and sent word around the world that Kansas is open for business."

Maine, Governor Paul LePage: "We have added an "Open for Business," sign to remind everyone that prosperity should also be a way of life here in Maine. A message that I hope will become the new sign of the times."
(The sign vanished two months later. "LePage spokeswoman Adrienne Bennett said, 'Whether or not the sign is up, we are open for business. It's unfortunate that some person or persons decided to take it upon themselves to take the sign down.' Asked whether the administration would replace the missing sign, Bennett replied: 'We have no intention of using taxpayer dollars to put up another sign. What we would like to see is this

8

sign put back.'"

Three months after that, the sign was replaced, the costs covered by a "group of businessmen." "After the theft, a tongue-in-cheek advertisement appeared briefly on Craigslist offering a "right-wing political sign" for $1,000. The ad said the seller would trade for a "multi-panel mural depicting the labor movement," a reference to a mural LePage removed from the state Labor Department.)

Michigan, Governor Rick Snyder: "The steps we're taking will make our state attractive to investors and entrepreneurs globally, and we want the world to know that Michigan is open for business."

New Mexico, Governor Susana Martinez: "It's the small businesses, the mom and pop shops, that get lost in the layers of red tape. We will help them and in doing so, send a loud message and a very clear message: New Mexico is open for business."

Ohio, Governor John Kasich: "Ohio's open for business. If you've had problems, it's a new day and a new way of doing things in Ohio."

Pennsylvania, Governor Tom Corbett: "My goal is to make Pennsylvania the standard of excellence . . . it's now time to come together, to tell the rest of the world that Pennsylvania is open for business."

South Carolina, Governor Nikki Haley: "South Carolina is open for business and when you get here we will take care of you."

Texas, Governor Rick Perry: "Come to Texas. We're wide open for business."

Wisconsin, Governor Scott Walker: "Wisconsin is open for business. In these challenging economic times while Illinois is raising taxes, we are lowering them. On my first day in office I called a special session of the legislature, not in order to raise taxes, but to open Wisconsin for business."

JAN BREWER, GOVERNOR OF ARIZONA

Governor Jan Brewer was born in Hollywood, California in 1944. Brewer attended Glendale Community College, receiving certification as a radiological technologist, before serving as an Arizona state senator and state representative. Brewer also served as chairman of the Maricopa Country Board of Supervisors before being elected as Secretary of State of Arizona in 2002. As Secretary of State, she became governor of Arizona in January 2009 after then-Governor Janet Napolitano left office to become President Barack Obama's Secretary of Homeland Security. Brewer was then elected to a full term in 2010 with 55% of the vote. Her book *Scorpions for Breakfast: My Fight Against Special Interests, Liberal Media, and Cynical Politicos to Secure America's Border* was published in 2011. One of Governor Brewer's best known initiatives, an immigration law (SB 1070) had three of its four provisions struck down by the Supreme Court in June 2012. Governor Brewer and her husband John have had three children, two of whom are still living.

"Well, we all know that the majority of the people that are coming to Arizona and trespassing are now becoming drug mules. They're coming across our borders in huge numbers. The drug cartels have taken control of the immigration. So they are criminals. They're breaking the law when they are trespassing and they're criminals when they pack the marijuana and the drugs on their backs . . . [Many are coming to the US to look for work but] are accosted, and they become subjects of the drug cartels." [1]

"We cannot afford all this illegal immigration and everything that comes with it. Everything from the crime to the drugs and the kidnappings and extortion and the beheadings and the fact that people can't feel safe in their communities." [2]

On boycotts of Arizona by other governments in response to Arizona's policy on illegal immigrants: "I think any reasonable person would understand that elected officials certainly don't encourage boycotting either a city or a county or another state, and particularly when another country is calling for the boycott, that you would support that other country. Aren't we all Americans? My goodness! I mean, it just doesn't make any kind of sense to me whatsoever. And it's - and it's disturbing. It's disheartening." [3]

"Bottom line is, is that, you know, Greta, you're a lawyer, I'm not, but you have five lawyers in a room, you're going to get five different opinions, generally speaking." [3]

"If the feds aren't going to do their job, well, then, I'm up to suing the feds to make them do their job! I mean, they sued Arizona, you know, we can sue them back! I mean, they're not - they're not enforcing the laws!" [3]

"It is . . . one of the hardest things I've had to become accustomed to . . . to not be able to go outside, jump in my car and go where I want." Discussing how having a chauffeur as governor has been an adjustment for her, and that the added security she now has has "clipped her wings"[4]

"The federal government today has involved itself in yet another instance of excessive and unnecessary regulation - this time, potentially at the expense of hundreds of high-paying jobs and billions of dollars' worth of revenue for the Arizona economy . . . If instituted, this uranium mining ban would deal a blow to future economic growth near the Grand Canyon, as well as our nation's attempts to improve its energy independence. That's because these sections of the Colorado Plateau contain the highest-grade uranium ore in the country . . . The responsible extraction of these deposits would assist domestic energy production and pump an estimated $10 billion into the local economy over the life of the mines, creating quality jobs in rural Arizona and tribal areas of our state hit hard by the recession."[5]

"I spent many a night sitting on my patio at 2 o'clock in the morning praying. It was a decision I deliberated on for a long time." On her decision that Arizona's budget deficit could not be closed without raising taxes. [6]

"I think he should get back to business being the president of the United States . . . I don't think his comic attitude and laughing at a serious issue is being very well received, certainly not here in Arizona, I would imagine not across America. This is a serious situation. And for him to go to a pep rally and make light of the situation is unbelievable." Reaction to President Obama's joke that some Republicans would not be happy with border policy until a border moat with alligators was added." [7]

"The courts couldn't sap SB 1070's strength as a rallying point for those of us sick and tired of hearing that our nation's border can't be secured, illegal immigration is just too big a problem to be solved or that we all must simply accept the drug smugglers on our soil and drophouses in our neighborhoods . . . Arizona's actions and the subsequent national attention that resulted has helped pressure the White House to act on border security in ways it never would have otherwise. Now, we must keep up the pressure." [8]

"As someone who was raised from the age of 10 by a widowed mother, I am well aware that single or unmarried individuals can make wonderful parents. This legislation merely establishes marital status of adoptive parents among a host of factors to be considered when placing a child." [9]

"The lawsuit to stop our prayer proclamations is nothing more than an attempt to drive religious expression from the public square. I intend to fight that lawsuit - vigorously - every step of the way." [10]

"I do not support designating one person as the gatekeeper to the ballot for a candidate, which could lead to arbitrary or politically motivated decisions. In addition, I never imagined being presented with a bill that could require candidates for president of the greatest and most powerful nation on Earth to submit their 'early baptismal or circumcision certificates' among other records to the Arizona secretary of state. This is a bridge too far." [11]

"This legislation is consistent with my strong track record of supporting common sense measures to protect the health of women and safeguard our most vulnerable population-the unborn." [12]

"This is a common-sense law that tightens existing state regulations and closes loopholes in order to ensure that taxpayer dollars are not used to fund abortions, whether directly or indirectly. By signing this measure into law, I stand with the majority of Americans who oppose the use of taxpayer funds for abortion."[15]

12

"I looked at it, as either it's the state of Arizona or it's my political career. And I chose the state of Arizona. Of course, at the time we knew - at least I knew - how bad it was going to be. Today I will tell you I wish it was as bad as I thought it was going to be (then), because it's only been worse . . . If you give anybody the information and the facts, you can do the math. I resisted, too. I didn't want to raise taxes. I mean, I kept pushing back with all my financial people." [13]

Reporter Brahm Resnik: "Is it fair that businesses should get these tax breaks while universities suffer and those patients suffer?"

Brewer: "Absolutely. Absolutely."

Resnik: "Because?"

Brewer: "Because it is business that drives our economy. It's business that allows people to have jobs. It's the jobs that allow people to spend the money and it's jobs that allow people to become and be self-responsible for themselves." [14]

"We know businesses, particularly high paying wage businesses, are the people who create those jobs and if you stymie them and you make it impossible for them to maintain here by charging them above their competitive states that we're competing with, they won't come here, they won't stay here, they will go someplace else and if we become competitive, they will bring new jobs, we will keep the jobs that we have, and that means that it's, [not] to use the phrase "the trickle down, the bottom line is that more people will have jobs, and therefore those people with the jobs are going to go out and it's going to trickle down to the lawnmower guy, to the dry cleaner, it's just the facts." [14]

"Mandating that a religious institution provide a service in direct contradiction with its faith would represent an obvious encroachment upon the First Amendment." [16]

SAM BROWNBACK, GOVERNOR OF KANSAS

Governor Sam Brownback was born in Parker, Kansas in 1956. In high school, he was elected the state president, and later national vice-president, of the Future Farmers of America. He was student body president at Kansas State University and graduated with a Bachelors' degree in Agricultural Economics. Brownback also was elected class president at the University of Kansas Law School, from which he graduated in 1982. He was the youngest Secretary of the Kansas Board of Agriculture in its history and co-authored two books on agricultural law while teaching part time at Kansas State. He was elected to the U. S. House in 1994 and took the United States Senate seat long occupied by Robert Dole in 1996. After finishing out Dole's term, he was elected to two more terms in the Senate. He was elected Governor in 2010 with 63% of the vote. Governor Brownback and his wife Mary have five children.

"I'm the first conservative governor in probably 50 years in Kansas." [1]

"May this Capitol radiate in your love. We pray that in Jesus' name. Amen." Praying at a prayer session in the former State Supreme Court Chambers at the start of the new legislative session. [2]

"[The Affordable Care Act's contraception coverage mandate is] an affront to people of faith . . . Freedom is a gift from God, not a privilege a government is entitled to take away. This unconscionable mandate must not be allowed to stand, and by your prayers and work, it will not be allowed to stand. Keep fighting for as long as it takes." [3]

"Both these bills reflect the culture of life that is being embraced all across Kansas. They represent a mainstream, bi-partisan and common sense approach to a divisive issue." Upon signing a bill into law placing new restrictions on abortions, including new restrictions on abortions after 22 weeks gestation and requiring two parents to sign off on abortions for minors. [4]

"The dignity of every individual in the state of Kansas, this country, the world has been significant to me for some time. Whether that's somebody in Africa, somebody in prison, somebody that is unborn. To sign major pro-life legislation in a first term, I think is important and significant." [5]

"These bills establish that Kansas, in the heart of America, is a culture-of-life state - and we're not going back." [6]

"God was merciful." Commenting after a deadly tornado outbreak that did extensive damage in Kansas, noting it could have been much worse. [7]

"It's important, it's key, it's happening in your world. You need to do something about it . . . I think what we really need to be doing nationally as a country right now, is focusing on policies that created pools of trafficking victims." [8]

"If the American people don't want Obamacare, it's a political issue, and it's about this fall presidential race, whether or not you want to implement it. I want to see what happens in the fall." Arguing Kansas shouldn't implement the ACA's health insurance exchanges until after the November 2012 election. [9]

"The states are to be the laboratory for democracy. Why not here and why not us and why not now? . . . We cannot continue on this path and hope we can move forward and win the future. It won't work. We have to change course, and we're going to have to be aggressive about it or we are doomed to a slow decline." [10]

"This is a modest, prudent measure. You show photo ID to cash a check, you show one to get on a plane, it's something people are used to doing, It's a modest and important measure to ensure the sanctity of the vote." On signing a bill into law that requires proof of citizenship to register to vote and photo identification at the polls to be able to vote. [11]

"My staff overreacted to this tweet, and for that I apologize. Freedom of speech is among our most treasured freedoms."-Statement apologizing for his staff's action in reporting a tweet criticizing the Governor written by a high school student in a Youth in Government program, leading in turn to the student being called into her principal's office and ordered to apologize to the governor. [12]

"We wanted to be a major animal state. We are. We wanted to be a major dairy state. We are. We've got the water. We've got the productive land. We've got the wind." [13] - Commenting on an agreement with Dannon that a Kansas dairy will be the exclusive supplier of milk to a Dannon yogurt plant in Texas. (The reporter notes the wind remark was made in jest, but that he did go on to note the development of wind power in Kansas.

"Three billion dollars of investment in wind has occurred in a 12-month time frame in my state. The [Production Tax Credit for wind energy] has worked." [14]

"This is a difficult job. And we're proposing a lot of change, and change is uncomfortable. But we are on a bad trajectory of what we have seen of job growth, of what we had seen in budgets in this state. We've got to get off this trajectory." [15]

"I believe this will be a more successful way for us to move forward. We'll be able to leverage and raise private dollars."-Arguing in favor of his plan to close the Kansas Arts Commission, which would make Kansas the first state to eliminate state funding of the arts. (He later proposed an alternative: merging the Arts Commission with the state Film Commission and restoring some funding). [16]

"We need to get to a pro-growth tax position. We've got the proposal there. It's queued up. It's paid for. We need to do it, and then we need to get a budget through that takes care of the needs of the state." [17]

"Twelve thousand new private-sector jobs over the last year. How about Kansas is going to be number one in new wind energy projects in 2012? Number one in the country. How about Kansas is in the bottom 11 in the country in unemployment rates?" [15]

"You have to have incentives nowadays to be competitive. It is a very competitive job market . . . You gotta go out and hustle and that's why [Kansas] moved from 51st in job creation, we were dead last a year ago, and went to 13th." [19]

[On what taxes he wants to be changed]: "Personal income is one that has the biggest focus on. I've made no secret of my thinking that our tax rates are too high. They're too high in the region. We bleed taxpayers to every other state in the region, except Nebraska. We need to get the rate down. We need to make ourselves competitive. And most economists will say that the best thing for your tax policy is to get it the lowest if you want growth to take place and to get social engineering out of your policies. If you want that building over there renovated, don't put it in your tax policy. Subsidize it directly, because your tax policy then affects how your overall economy performs. This will be the way that most economists would look at and say, 'That's the way you ought to do it.'"[18]

"Almost every economist would say to you, if you want to create growth, and you're a competitive state, you've got to get your state personal income tax rates down, and your fastest growing states are the ones with no personal income tax." [20]

"I'm gonna grow any way we can." [19]

"From a high tax state to a low tax state. From a state struggling to pay our day-to-day bills to a state with a healthy bank account. From issuing more bonds and borrowing from our kids to paying down our debt." [21]

"Our state has gone through an incredible transition in just two years: from a projected $500 million deficit to putting nearly half a billion dollars in the bank . . . A $1 billion swing can only occur when we commit ourselves to shrinking the footprint of state government and pursuing policies that grow the economy." [22]

"We will have pro-growth tax reform in Kansas this year that will create tens of thousands of jobs and will make our state the best place in America to start and grow a small business." Preparing to sign a bill featuring deep tax cuts. [23]

"What is it we still need to do in state government? If we don't need to do it, then let's not do it." [24]

"I want to look at all of [the Education budget]. This is all negotiations. I would much rather see them add it on a target. We've got a 4th-grade reading problem. Let's target this to testing and reading rather than just, here's a big dollop, here's more resources." [25]

"I despise the issue of this being resolved by the courts. I think some people in the past have said this is kind of the easier political route to resolve-let the courts do it. That is not what should happen." On a lawsuit filed by a group of school districts protesting cuts in state aid. [24]

"Stopping ObamaCare is now in the hands of the American people. It begins with electing a new president this fall." One-line statement following the Supreme Court ruling on the ACA. [26]

"As I traveled the state during the last few years, one resounding concern I heard from elected leaders and our fellow Kansans was the impact and burden of unnecessary, outdated or duplicative regulations. That's why Lt. Governor-Elect Jeff Colyer and I pledged to establish an Office of the Repealer within existing resources to streamline state laws and regulations." [27]

"That one didn't go so well. So I don't know if anybody wants my endorsement." Regarding his support for Texas Gov. Rick Perry in Fall 2011. [28]

"The birth of the United States was a watershed moment in human history. Our founding fathers created this nation based on liberty, light and hope. As Americans, it remains our duty to be a beacon of hope for liberty-loving peoples across the globe. 236 years after the signing of the Declaration of Independence, we sometimes take for granted the enormous challenges that lay ahead of our founding fathers those summer days in 1776. Every generation since has faced, and overcome its challenges through the strength and courage of the American people. Today too we face enormous challenges, but the hard work, dedication and patriotism will make our country even stronger for our future generations. God Bless America. Have a happy and safe Fourth of July." [29]

"Our goal is for our economy to look more like Texas, and a lot less like California." [30]

CHRIS CHRISTIE, GOVERNOR OF NEW JERSEY

Governor Chris Christie was born in Newark, New Jersey in 1962 and was raised in Livingston, New Jersey. He graduated from the University of Delaware in 1984 with a degree in political science and went on to earn his J.D. from Seton Hall University School of Law in 1987. Christie served as a Freeholder in Morris County, practiced law, and, for several years, was a lobbyist. From 2002-2008, Christie was United States Attorney in New Jersey, a position in which he won numerous prosecutions in public corruption cases. He was elected governor in 2009 with 49% of the vote, defeating incumbent Democrat Jon Corzine. Governor Christie and his wife Mary have four children.

"I don't believe those of you in this room who voted for me elected me to run a charm school. I believe in the last eight months, I have proven you right." [1]

"Our state is in crisis. Our people are hurting. Now is the time when we all must resist the traditional, selfish call to protect your own turf at the cost of our state. It is time to leave the corner, join the sacrifice, come to the center of the room and be part of the solution." [2]

"Today, we come to terms with the fact that we cannot spend money on everything we want. Today, the days of Alice in Wonderland budgeting in Trenton end." [2]

"I take no joy in having to make these decisions. I know these judgments will affect fellow New Jerseyans and will hurt. This is not a happy moment. However, what choices do we have left? The defenders of the status quo will start chattering as soon as I leave this chamber. They'll say the problems are not that bad; listen to me, I can spare you the pain and sacrifice. We know this is simply not true. New Jersey has been steaming toward financial disaster for years due to that kind of attitude. The people elected us to end the talk and to act decisively. Today is the day for the complaining to end and for statesmanship to begin." [2]

"The special interests have already begun to scream their favorite word, which, coincidentally, is my nine year old son's favorite word when we are making him do something he knows is right but does not want to do-'unfair' . . . And make no mistake: our priorities are to reduce and reform New Jersey's habit of excessive government spending, to reduce taxes, to encourage job creation, to shrink our bloated government, and to fund our responsibilities on a pay-as-you-go basis and not leave them for future generations. In short, to make New Jersey a home for growth instead of a fiscal basket case." [2]

"I'm going to Illinois. I mean soon. I'm going to Illinois, personally, and going to start talking to businesses in Illinois and get them to come to New Jersey." [3]

"Evolution is required teaching. If there's a certain school district that also wants to teach creationism, that's not something we should decide in Trenton." [On whether he believes in evolution or creationism], "that's none of your business . . . I think it's really a dangerous area for a governor who stands up from the top of the state to say you should teach this, you shouldn't teach that." [4]

"You know, at some point there has to be parity. There has to be parity between what is happening in the real world, and what is happening in the public sector world." [5]

"These are the typical kind of scare tactics that they involve themselves in. Scaring students in the classroom, scaring parents with the notes home in the bookbags, and the mandatory 'Project Democracy Homework' asking your parents about what they're going to do in the school board election, and reporting back to your teachers union representatives, using the students like drug mules to carry information back to the classroom, is reprehensible." Regarding the New Jersey Education Association. [6]

"I said all during the campaign last year that I was going to govern as if I was a one-termer. And everybody felt that it was just stuff you say during a campaign to sound good. I think after the first 12 weeks, given the stuff I've done, they figure: 'He's just crazy enough to do it.'" [7]

"I'm a product of public schools in New Jersey, and I have great admiration for people who commit their lives to teaching, but this isn't about them. This is about a union president who makes $265,000 a year, and her executive director who makes $550,000 a year. This is about a union that has been used to getting its way every time. And they have intimidated governors for the last 30 years." [7]

"See what happens when you're not looking? Snuck right up on ya." On telling former New York Governor Pataki that New Jersey's taxes are higher than New York's. [7]

"I just think that we're at a point in our economic life here in our state - and - and, candidly, across the country, where increased taxes is just the wrong way to go. The people of our state are not convinced that state government, county government, local government has done all they can with the money we already give them, rather than the money that we have before." [8]

"Ignorance is behind the criticism of Sohail Mohammed. [He] is an extraordinary American who is an outstanding lawyer and played an integral role in the post-September 11 period in building bridges between the Muslim American community in this state and law enforcement. I was there for it. I saw it personally. And the folks who criticize my appointment of Sohail Mohammed are ignorant, absolutely ignorant of that, and they are criticizing him because he's a Muslim-American and because he represented people who were inappropriately detained by the FBI post-9/11." [9]

"Sharia law has nothing to do with this at all. It's crazy. It's crazy. The guy's an American citizen who has been an admitted lawyer to practice in the state of New Jersey, swearing an oath to uphold the laws of New Jersey, the constitution of the state of New Jersey, and the Constitution of the United States of America . . . This sharia law business is crap. It's just crazy. And I'm tired of dealing with the crazies." [10]

"They don't pay me enough not to have fun, you know? . . . And I say listen, this is a perfect job for me. We got no place to go but up if we have the guts to do the hard things and over the last two years, we have done the hard things, we've held the line on taxes, now we are going to cut taxes." [11]

"And let me tell you what the truth is. What's the truth that no one is talking about, here is the truth that no one is talking about: you're going to have to raise the retirement age for Social Security. Oh I just said it and I'm still standing here! I did not vaporize into the carpeting and I said it! We have to reform Medicare because it costs too much and it is going to bankrupt us. Once again lightning did not come through the windows and strike me dead." [12]

"See, one of things that the public sector unions don't understand about my approach in New Jersey is that they think I'm attacking them. I'm attacking the leadership of the union. Because they're greedy and they're selfish and self-interested." [12]

"You know there's a lot of talk now about partisanship and the negative, angry tone in some of our political debates. And there is a time and a place for partisanship, I absolutely believe in that. And so did our founding fathers, they believed in partisanship . . . They believed in vigorous debate and so do I. It's the nature of our country based on our founding to have principled disagreements among people of good will and I'm not disagreeing with folks just for sake of disagreeing. And I'm not fighting for the sake of fighting. I fight for the things that matter. I save my energy for the fights of consequence. And as a result, some people say I'm too combative, some people say I'm too much of a fighter. Well I'll tell you I'm fighting now because now is the time that matters most for New Jersey's future and in America's future." [12]

"He should just write a check and shut up. Really, and just contribute. The fact of the matter is that I'm tired of hearing about it. If he wants to give the government more money, he's got the ability to write a check - go ahead and write it . . . I'm not going to get into this class warfare business where certain people are more important than others or deserves more . . . Everyone deserves to have the government responsive to their concerns and needs." Responding to media coverage of Warren Buffett's argument that he and his fellow wealthiest Americans should pay more in taxes. [13]

"You have numb nuts like Reed Gusciora who put out a statement comparing me to George Wallace and Lester Maddox. Now, come on guys, at some point, you've got to able to call BS on those kind of press releases." Responding to criticism from an advocate for same-sex marriage who wrote a press release stating, "Govs. Lester Maddox and George Wallace would have found allies in Chris Christie over efforts by the Justice Department to end segregation in the South." [14]

"Somebody's going down tonight, but it ain't gonna be jobs, sweetheart." To a female heckler who said that jobs were going down in New Jersey under Christie. [15]

"Hey . . . you know what, first of all it's none of your business. I don't ask you where you send your kids to school. Don't bother me where I send mine." Responding to a woman on a public television show where he was the featured guest who asked him "You don't send your children to public schools. You send them to private schools, so I was wondering why you think it's fair to be cutting funding to public schools?" [16]

"You know I saw some of these news feeds upstairs of people sitting on the beach on Asbury Park. Get the hell off the beach in Asbury Park and get out. You're done. It's 4:30, you've maximized your tan. Get off the beach." Urging people to leave the beach before Hurricane Irene. [17]

"Well then what the hell are we paying you for?" Criticizing President Barack Obama for not doing more to help the budget "supercommittee" come to an agreement. [18]

"That kind of intolerance is something I think is unacceptable. So I don't have any problem with him being fired. You've got to make decisions in this job. I made one." On not blocking the firing of a NJ Transit employee for burning a Koran at a political protest. [19]

"Don't worry, Jesse, people gave plenty of reasons why I couldn't be governor, though being too small wasn't one of them." Responding to a YouTube video of 5 year old Jesse Koczon who said he was "too small" to be governor. Christie made the boy honorary Governor of New Jersey for a day and gave him and his family a private meeting and tour of the Governor's office. [20]

"I would love to show these people who say that because I'm overweight that means I'm not disciplined. They think you could get to where I am and be undisciplined? Let me show them." [21]

"[President Obama] is as good a politician as I've ever seen. I think where the shortcoming has been is in governing." [21]

"All the [teachers' unions in New Jersey] care about is increasing their membership and keeping their membership enslaved to them. " [21]

"I'm not going to send the income tax money of New Jerseyans to cities in distress unless I can ensure them we have the oversight that's necessary that that money will be spent wisely and not wasted." [26]

"Whitney Houston was an important part of the cultural fabric of this state. She was a cultural icon in this state and her accomplishments in her life were a source of great pride for many people in this state and for this state as a whole. On that basis, I think she's entitled to have that recognition made for her." [22] On the decision to fly flags at half mast after Houston's death.

"I am disturbed by people who believe that because Whitney Houston's ultimate demise - and we don't know what is the cause of her death yet - but because of her history of substance abuse that somehow she's forfeited the good things that she did in her life. I just reject that on a human level . . . What I would say to everybody is there but for the grace of God go I." [23]

"An across the board tax cut is fair - every New Jersey taxpayer will benefit. Every New Jerseyan's rates will go down. Every New Jerseyan will see relief. This is exactly what I was talking about when I took office; that the tough choices would lead to the right ones. Let's face it: more money does not necessarily lead to a better education." [24].

"Our economy suffers while Washington politicians - in both parties - fiddle. Over the last two years New Jersey did the exact opposite. We achieved results because we did it together." [25]

"Over the last two years, New Jersey is now seen around the country once again, not exclusively as the butt of late-night jokes, but as a focus of the evening news and Sunday talk shows. Why? Because, once again, we are leading America - by taking on the big things in public policy." [25]

"We're missing the boat in terms of how we can help these folks turn their lives around. We need to have a broader, more effective program for reentry after people pay their debt to society." Speaking at the Cathedral Kitchen in Camden, NJ which teaches ex-offenders cooking skills to help them find employment. [27]

"Every human being is one of God's creatures and deserves the love and respect that God gives to all of us. What we need to do each and every day is to live our lives in a way that encourages everyone to understand why this cause is so important . . . As long as I have the honor of serving as governor of this state, you will know you have someone sitting in that office who understands this issue, who appreciates it, and who will continue to stand up and speak strongly in favor of the protection of human life - of every human life - in New Jersey." [33]

Christie to William Brown, a law student, former Democratic legislative candidate and former Navy SEAL at Rutgers-Camden Law School who was heckling him: "And let me tell you something. If after you graduate from law school you conduct yourself like that in a courtroom, your rear end's going to be thrown in jail, idiot." After the student was led away by police, Christie said, "I tried to be patient with the guy; every time I tried to answer he started yelling over again. Look, damn, man, I'm governor, could you just shut up for a second?"

Later, Christie said, "I honor his service . . . [but] just because he was a Navy SEAL doesn't give him the right to be a jerk . . . Every time I tried to answer, he yelled or started to interrupt, he did it four times . . . his is a guy with a political agenda who came in and wanted to try and make me look bad. I'm not a heavy bag. I have arms too. You want to punch me, I'll punch you back." [28]

"[Newt Gingrich has been] an embarrassment for the [Republican] Party . . . I'm not talking about character, I'm talking about how you conducted yourself in office. Newt Gingrich has embarrassed the party over time - whether he'll do it again in the future, I don't know." [29]

"We're not going to listen to partisan hacks like [Senator] Frank Lautenberg. He should be ashamed of himself." [30]

"[The story is] completely ridiculous . . . [it is] a bunch of research and a conspiracy theory in search of a story . . . I don't even know these people, and I've never had any interaction with them." [31] Commenting on a report that his education proposals closely followed a template from ALEC, the American Legislative Exchange Council.

"I've never seen a less optimistic time in my lifetime in this country. And people wonder why. I think it's really simple: It's because government's now telling them to stop dreaming, stop striving, we'll take care of you. We're turning into a paternalistic entitlement society. That will not just bankrupt us financially; it will bankrupt us morally . . . When the American people no longer believe that this is a place where only their willingness to work hard and to act with honor and integrity and ingenuity determines their success in life, then we'll have a bunch of people sitting on a couch waiting for their next government check." [32]

"I mean can you guys please take the bat out on her for once? The hypocrisy meter has got to tilt on her." Urging the media to label Democratic State Senator Loretta Weinberg, a 76 year old widow, a hypocrite for her criticism of his pension policies. [36]

"I'm not going to the Nets game tonight and my message to the Nets is goodbye. If you don't want to stay, we don't want you. Seriously, I'm not going to be in the business of begging people to stay here. That's one of the most beautiful arenas in America that they've had a chance to play in. It's in one of the country's most vibrant cities. They want to leave here and go to Brooklyn? Good riddance. See you later." Speaking on the day of the last New Jersey Nets basketball game in the Garden State before moving to Brooklyn. [34]

"If conservative values can work in New Jersey, conservative values can work in Wisconsin and every other corner of America . . . Here's what the people of Wisconsin needed to be reminded of: Scott Walker stands with you. When tens of thousands of people crowded your statehouse, disrupted your government and tried to scare Scott Walker, Scott Walker stood with you . . . When the moneyed special interests from Washington, D.C., descended into the state of Wisconsin to try to sell fear over courage, Scott Walker stood with you. And now, as they try to do nothing less than to reverse the overwhelming democratic election of the leader of this state, you know Scott Walker, you know his principles, you know what he stands for."Speaking to a rally in Wisconsin [35]

"The war on drugs, while well-intentioned, has been a failure. We're warehousing addicted people everyday in state prisons in New Jersey, giving them no treatment . . . If you're pro-life, as I am, you can't be pro-life just in the womb. Every life is precious and every one of God's creatures can be redeemed, but they won't if we ignore them . . . It costs us $49,000 a year to warehouse a prisoner in New Jersey state prisons last year. A full year of inpatient drug treatment costs $24,000 a year." [37]

"First of all, I was glad that the Supreme Court ruled that extortion is still illegal in America - and that's a relief because Obamacare, on Medicaid to the states, was extortion. [A provision of the Affordable Care Act said] 'you expand your program to where we tell you, and if you don't, we're taking the rest of your money away.' That's extortion. It was a whole bunch of nice words in a bill, but it was extortion. I'm really glad that a majority of the Supreme Court still supports the notion, as a former prosecutor, that extortion is still illegal, even when done by the president of the United States." [38]

"Did I say on topic? Are you stupid? On topic, on topic. Next question." Speaking to a reporter, who asked him, "Governor, on Monday are you going to be addressing the legislature?" After the reporter tried to follow-up, Governor Christie said, "Thank you all very much, and I'm sorry for the idiot over there. Take care," and walked off. [39]

Reporter Jeffrey Goldberg: "Do you think Mitt Romney could relate to this? To a Bruce Springsteen show?"

Governor Chris Christie: "No one is beyond the reach of Bruce! No one is beyond the reach of Bruce!"

Goldberg: "What about Newt?"

Christie: "He's been married three times! He'd get this. You know what I mean?" [40]

TOM CORBETT, GOVERNOR OF PENNSYLVANIA

Governor Tom Corbett was born in Philadelphia, Pennsylvania in 1949. He graduated from Lebanon Valley College and taught high school civics and history one year. In 1975, he earned his law degree from St. Mary's University School of Law. Corbett served in the Pennsylvania Army National Guard from 1971-1984, rising to the rank of Captain. In 1988, Corbett was appointed by President George H. W. Bush as U.S. Attorney for the Western District of Pennsylvania. After the election of President Bill Clinton, Corbett returned to private practice. From 1995-1997, Corbett was the State Attorney General, filling the unexpired term of Attorney General Ernie Preate. Between 1997 and 2007, Corbett worked as an attorney, first as an assistant general counsel for Waste Management, Inc., then opening up his own firm, Thomas Corbett & Associates. Corbett was elected as Pennsylvania's Attorney General in November of 2004 and reelected in 2008. He was elected Governor of Pennsylvania in 2010 with 52% of the vote. Governor Corbett and his wife Susan Manbeck have two children.

"The jobs are there, but if we keep extending unemployment, people are just going to sit there. I've literally had construction companies tell me, 'I can't get people to come back to work until - they say, 'We'll come back when unemployment runs out." [1]

"I've brought somebody who's qualified, who knows what he's doing. He was president of the association of turnpike executives at one point in time. So on paper he's a very qualified person if you just take out the part that he's the father of my campaign manager." [2]

"[We] have to change the culture of this place. It means we stop the one-time fixes and gimmicks that have barely held the machine of government together. It's time to peel off the duct tape and get to work on what's broken underneath." [3]

"If we do the hard things necessary when we are in a windless spot on this ocean, the breeze that is sure to follow will move us all the faster . . . In many ways what we need to do is the same as reviving an abandoned apple tree. If the tree isn't tended and the branches pruned, that tree will grow into a tangle of limbs and leaves. But it will bear no fruit. We need to take this tree, so long overgrown, and cut back what isn't fruitful. And we need to do that essential pruning on all branches of government. We need to do the hard cutting so the tree can once again bear fruit. And that fruit is jobs." [3]

"Today's ruling by the Supreme Court to uphold President Obama's health-care law is disappointing. If implemented, we will be saddled with a nearly $2 trillion entitlement." [4]

"Just as the oil companies decided to headquarter in one of a dozen states with oil . . . let's make Pennsylvania the Texas of the natural gas boom." [3]

"Nothing we build in stone and mortar can sufficiently honor the deeds" [of the passengers of Flight 93 on Sept. 11, 2001] . . . "I get a feeling when I go to some of those places, to Gettysburg, to the Alamo and here, a feeling of spirit, of a presence . . . But the truth is this location is like no other. There is nothing with which to compare the passenger uprising of ten years ago." [5]

"We need to think smarter about how and when and how long to jail people. We need to be tough on crime but we also need to consider the fiscal implications of our prison system . . . We also can't afford to ask counties in our state to subsist on a prison-based economy. We need industries that generate wealth, not sorrow." [3]

"Two hundred years ago a group of English poets talked of building a utopian community along the banks of the Susquehanna. It was their dream to come to Penn's Woods and flourish. They never made it here. Maybe they heard about our property taxes." [3]

"We will not raise taxes. There is no talking around these limits. Every dollar taken in tax is one less in the hands of a job holder or job creator." [11]

"Nothing we build in stone and mortar can sufficiently honor the deeds" [of the passengers of Flight 93 on Sept. 11, 2001] . . . "I get a feeling when I go to some of those places, to Gettysburg, to the Alamo and here, a feeling of spirit, of a presence . . . But the truth is this location is like no other. There is nothing with which to compare the passenger uprising of ten years ago." [5]

"As to the actions of Mr. [Joe] Paterno, the attorney general made a determination that he had not at this point in time done anything that would be of a criminal nature. But in my opinion, when you don't follow through, when you don't continue on to make sure that actions are taken, then I lose confidence in your ability to lead. That would be the case here . . . In looking at other cases like this, it would not be uncommon to find other victims, because when the word gets out, when people understand that authorities are actually doing something about this, that they may be believed, then more people come forward in other investigations. If I'm to speculate, I wouldn't be surprised if we had more victims come forward. That's why the attorney and the state police have put up numbers for people to call if they've been a victim." [6]

"We are set to start work on one of the most important jobs state government can do, and that is to rearrange our priorities when it comes to education. It needs to be: child, parent, teacher . . . and just in that order . . . We can't guarantee their success, but we owe all students a fighting chance . . . We're talking about our children and we owe it to them to reform the system . . . Some students are consigned to failure because of their ZIP codes. They live in the shadow of failing public schools they must attend because their families lack the resources or ability to enroll them elsewhere . . . Opportunity scholarships provide additional choices for Pennsylvania students." [7]

"I'm calling on the employees of our public schools - administrators, teachers, support workers, everyone - to hold the line. If it means a pay freeze, trust me, you'll have plenty of company out there to keep you warm." [3]

"We're here because we can't continue down the same path and think that we're going to get a different result. We have to think and act smarter. We have to have the will to do better . . . This is a long-term investment. This is an investment in these children, that when they're our age, we have drastically reduced the dropout rate and as a result, I believe, hopefully reduced quite a bit the client rate in Pennsylvania of people we take care of because we didn't give them a good education in the first place. So anybody that's looking for instant results, that's not going to happen." [8]

"We must tax no more, because the people have no more to give." [9]

"There has been much pressure to tax the gas being drawn from the Marcellus Shale. The Marcellus is a resource, a source of potential wealth, the foundation of a new economy. Not just something new to tax." [9]

"This growing industry will provide new career opportunities that will give our children a reason to stay here in Pennsylvania. Thanks to this legislation, this natural resource will safely and fairly fuel our generating plants and heat our homes while creating jobs and powering our state's economic engine for generations to come." Statement upon signing the Marcellus Shale bill into law. [10]

"We have to spend less. Because we have less to spend. This budget sorts the must-haves from the nice-to-haves." [9]

"If our country is a living body, these rivers are its veins. They connect our cities through industry. That's why we need to maintain them, to develop them, to recognize them as the lifeline they are. These rivers aren't just flowing bodies of water. They are a ceaseless creator of jobs." [12]

"Tax increases choke growth. Every credible study on the subject has taught us this: the states that have grown the fastest, attracted the most jobs, have stayed out of the way. If you tax less, people will see the point in earning more. If you regulate more sensibly, businesses will be able to maneuver in the turns of tight economies. The third reason not to increase taxes is pretty simple. The voters said no." [13]

"Welfare does not produce wealth." [14]

"I completely disagree. This is no barrier to voting. You have to have a photo ID to go anywhere." Responding to allegations that requiring voters to show ID was a partisan effort designed to suppress Democratic votes. [15]

"This [voter ID law] is a law of prevention. It is to prevent voter fraud. And I believe it needs to be prevented." [16]

"You will never hear me say 'impossible.' To say it, or worse, to believe it, would accomplish nothing. I see the possible. And in the possible I see a promising future for Pennsylvania." [17]

"As we open this new chapter in Pennsylvania's history, let us also step forward firmly dedicated to a civil discourse. Let us not confuse acrimony with passion or partisanship with principle. Rather, let us take this opportunity to begin a new kind of debate - one that honors our shared history and unites us as citizens in common purpose." [17]

"You just have to close your eyes." About his support for a bill that requires an ultrasound procedure prior to performing an abortion. [18]

NIKKI HALEY, GOVERNOR OF
SOUTH CAROLINA

Governor Nikki Haley was born in Bamberg, South Carolina in 1972. She is the first woman to serve as governor of South Carolina and the second Indian-American governor in the country. The daughter of Indian immigrants, she graduated from Clemson University with a degree in accounting and joined the FCR Corporation as an accounting supervisor. In 1994 she went on to work in her family business Exotica International, an upscale clothing firm, which later grew into a multi-million dollar company. Haley was the treasurer of the National Association of Women Business Owners in 2003 and became president in 2004. She served in the South Carolina House of Representatives from 2005-2010. In 2010, despite allegations of affairs, Haley won the Republican nomination and then was elected governor with 51% of the vote. Her autobiography, published in 2012, is *Can't Is Not an Option: My American Story*. Governor Haley and her husband Michael have two children.

"It's funny. Despite all the success the Tea Party has had in changing the subject in Washington from 'How do we spend more of the taxpayers' money?' to 'How do we stop digging ourselves into a bottomless pit of debt?' the press continues to ask me if the Tea Party is dying. Wishful thinking, I guess. My response is always 'Are you kidding me? We're just getting started!' I love the Tea Party. They're the reason people are getting energized about their government and elected officials all across the country are getting scared. It's a beautiful thing!" [1]

"What he said was absolutely unfortunate. Here you've got Representative Ryan trying to bring common sense to this world of insanity, and Newt absolutely cut him off at the knees. When you have a conservative fighting for real change, the last thing we need is a presidential candidate cutting him off at the knees." Reacting to Newt Gingrich's criticism of Rep. Paul Ryan's proposed Medicare plan. [2]

"We knew from the beginning it was us versus the establishment. We were settling [in South Carolina] for a Republican House, a Republican Senate, a Republican governor. I won't stop until we get a conservative House, a conservative Senate, a conservative governor." [3]

On the new voter ID law: "Find me those people who think that this is invading their rights - find - and I will go take them to the DMV myself and help them get that picture ID." [4]

"God bless that little girl at the "Post and Courier." Her job is to try and create conflict. My job is to create jobs." Responding on the "Laura Ingraham Show" to an article written by 25-year old *Post and Courier* reporter Renee Dudley questioning the value of a trip Haley took to Europe Haley said was to produce "jobs, jobs, jobs" for South Carolina. [5]

"I challenge individuals to drive through their communities and take a look at the areas that need change. Let's then join together to make that change, so we can attract industries to our communities." [6]

"By helping the organization you are helping your neighbor. This is getting back to neighbors taking care of neighbors in South Carolina, and not using government to do it, but using compassion to do it." Announcing an "Original Six Foundation" day to assist Allendale County. [7]

"My takeaway was here is a president who's saying we could be doing more on education, here is a president saying give more money to education, but this is also a president that is not untying any of the strings that come with the federal mandates. Enough of the talk, and now it is time for action . . . He's constantly telling us what we should spend on, but he's not allowing us the ability to do it. We constantly have to deal with these Medicaid budgets, but he's not giving us the flexibility to do that." Speaking at the Republican Governors Association after meeting with President Obama with other governors at the White House. [8]

"Pres. Obama is now telling SC that we can't enforce our illegal immigration laws. I'm trying to govern a state and the President keeps getting in my way. I will continue to fight him every step of the way." [10]

"Just as we should not relinquish control of education to the Federal government, neither should we cede it to the consensus of other states. Our children deserve swift action and the passage of a clean resolution that will allow our state to reclaim control of and responsibility for educating South Carolinians." Arguing for removing South Carolina from participation in "Common Core" educational standards. [9]

"At the end of the day when we all come together, I cannot continue to lead South Carolina with President Obama in office. I can't . . . President Obama is the hardest part about my job and he has to go." [11]

"Hands down, the biggest surprise I have had as governor is how much the federal government won't let me do my job. From health care to illegal immigration to job-killing regulations, we have a president and a Washington, D.C., crowd that think they know better than we do. Not only that, but they think there's a one-size-fits-all answer to all our problems, as if South Carolina were the same as California or Michigan." [12]

"Right next to that sign that is being mandated by Barack Obama's union cheerleaders at the NLRB [notifying workers that they have a right to unionize], I encourage all S.C. employers to put up another sign: in our state, every worker has the freedom to reject the efforts to form unions and keep their paychecks for themselves and their families instead of paying dues to union bosses in Washington." [13]

"South Carolina continues to be one of the lowest union participation states in the country. The reason is that our companies understand that they have to take care of those that take care of them. Our employees appreciate the direct honest relationship that they have with their employers. It will continue to be a winning combination." [14]

"Stand with me and help fight back now against the bullying of Liberal unions! Donate here: http://www.nikkihaley.com/splash/blfb/" [15]

"The biggest recruitment tool you could ever give me is to be able to go out and say that the corporate income tax is being phased out . . . I'm always amazed by the people that say, 'If you cut, where is the money going to come from?' If you ask these guys, any of the business people, if we cut taxes, they will increase revenues, they will hire more people, and you will turn the economy. You can ask someone who went to school in economics. That's the fundamental rule: Give them cash, and they will spend it turning the economy. This tax relief will continue to give more and more by revenue; it will give more and more by jobs." [16]

"I just signed into law a bill that will reduce taxes for small businesses from 5% to 3%! My focus is on jobs in our state which includes taking care of the businesses we already have. South Carolina will continue to improve our business environment in spite of President Obama and his tax hikes!" [17]

"You may see shopping bags. All I see is jobs, jobs, jobs, and that's what we love to see in South Carolina." At a grand reopening of a Tanger Outlet Center in Bluffton, SC, March 2011. [18]

"South Carolina will NOT expand Medicaid, or participate in any health exchanges. We will not support Pres. Obama's tax increase or job killing agenda. I WILL do everything I can to get Mitt Romney elected and work to strengthen our Senate so that we can repeal this un-American policy aimed at moving our country in the wrong direction." Reacting to the Supreme Court ruling on the Affordable Care Act on Facebook; capital letters are in the original. [19]

"I am proud of all of our Republican candidates. But we have a real problem when we have Republicans talking like dang Democrats against the free market. We believe in free markets." [20]

"[Sarah Palin] is the one person in this country who has taught every person in this state and this country what it means to use the power of your voice and what it means to understand that government needs to work for the people again." [21]

"Enough is enough. At what point can I go face any state in the country and say, 'We have a Republican House and we have a Republican Senate but we can't get tax reform in this state?' Something is very wrong."[22]

"Sorry fellas. I'm not going anywhere no matter how many lies you put on a blog. The days of dirty blogger politics will come to an end when people stop paying these guys to spread trash." [23]

"My faith in Christ has a profound impact on my daily life and I look to Him for guidance with every decision I make. God has blessed my family in so many ways and my faith in the Lord gives me great strength on a daily basis. Being a Christian is not about words, but about living for Christ every day." [24]

"We love fighters. We love fighters that understand that when it gets hot you keep moving and you fight for the good of the people. And that's what [Scott Walker]'s done." [26]

"I am the mother of an 11-year old daughter, and I believe that the best decisions for her are made by my husband and me. I believe the same is true for every child in this state. It is that belief that led me to vote to kill this bill - and it is the same reason I will oppose any government mandates on vaccines, whether they be for HPV, H1N1, or any other."-On her opposition to a cervical cancer prevention bill that did not feature a provision allowing parents to opt out. [24]

"I love that we are one of the least unionized states in the country. It is an economic development tool unlike any other." [25]

"We will protect the right of every private and public citizen to refuse to join a union, and, by executive order, I will make it clear that our state will not subsidize striking workers by paying them unemployment benefits." [25]

"When you are married with an army fella you sometimes have to watch military movies and so we are . . . *Act of Valor*. At least we have popcorn!!" [27]

"The kids are learning that chores apply in a Governor's mansion as well." [28]

"We are declaring October Bullying Prevention Month in South Carolina. I will be touring middle schools across the state this month to remind kids that bullying is not cool. Please take time to talk with your children about respecting others regardless of the differences." [29]

"Michael and I want to take this opportunity to thank the men and women of our military and their families for their courage, strength, and sacrifice they have given our country. While we celebrate you today, we, as a military family, honor you every day. May God bless our veterans and their families. And may He continue to bless the United States of America." [30]

"I appreciate freedom of speech. I do not appreciate mattresses on the grounds, urinating in the bushes and damage of state property. Occupiers were given until 6:00 to move off the property. They are welcome to picket during daylight hours. We respect the Rule of Law in South Carolina." Referring to Occupy protesters. [31]

"[Unions] will do everything they can to invade our state and drive a wedge between our workers and our employers. We can't have that. Unions thrive in the dark. Secrecy is their greatest ally, sunlight their most potent adversary." [25]

"We continue to get celebrity requests to interview Susan Smith, the woman who received national attention for drowning her children in a lake and lying about it in 1994. I will continue to DENY any access to her because she does not deserve the additional attention she craves and the family of her children have suffered enough. South Carolina has moved beyond that tragedy. " (capitals in the original). [32]

"We don't have unions in South Carolina because we don't need unions in South Carolina." [25]

"We're going to continue to be union busters in South Carolina." [33]

"I just want the truth out there, because I know I've done nothing wrong . . . [My accuser John Rainey was]"demeaning and demanding" [and told her that he wanted to] "prove certain things so when I took the oath they wouldn't find out later my family was related to terrorists. I'm still very offended by that. [He is a] racist, sexist bigot . . . " [34]

[On videotape of political opponents using a baseball bat to hit a pinata decorated with her face and her anti-union quotation]: "It's creepy! I still hurt every time I see it. But . . . this is not typical of South Carolinians. This is typical of union thugs . . . But all it does is it makes my heels taller, my heels sharper so that I can kick harder. I'm not going to stop beating up on the unions." [35]

"I'm not going to stop beating up on the Democrats for wasteful spending. And I'm going to keep on fighting for the things I fight for . . . There's a reason South Carolina's the new 'it' state and it's because we're a union buster and it's because we continue to be fiscally responsible and business-friendly. And there's nothing the Democrats or the unions can do to make me change that." [35]

"We're going to fight the unions and I needed a partner to help me do it." On naming Catherine Templeton, a labor attorney with a union-fighting reputation to head the state's labor and licensing agency. [37]

"Barack Obama doesn't appreciate right-to-work states. Mitt Romney appreciates right-to-work states. I need a partner in the White House." [38]

"I will not sign or support a casino in [the Bluffton region] or anywhere else in South Carolina. We are focused on bringing manufacturing and industry to every part of the state." [39]

"The interesting thing was [Mitt Romney] was one of the only governors that showed courage when it came to dealing with health care. I think that we are looking for a leader that's willing to, one, make courageous stands, take strong policy decisions, but two, also admit when a mistake was made." [41]

––––––––––––––––

"Dear Friend,

Yesterday a disturbing video was released of the South Carolina AFL-CIO President taking a swing at a piñata with my image on it. Please take a moment to watch the video here.

We're for civility in politics, the kind of civility President Obama has called for many times both before and since his inauguration.

His allies in Big Labor are obviously not. They have tried to bully South Carolina businesses with Boeing and the NLRB, they have tried to silence me through frivolous lawsuits, and now this.

What is just as disturbing is the double standard in the mainstream media. Can you imagine the outrage if this was a Tea Party activist and the piñata had President Obama's image on it? It would not be right in those circumstances, and it is not right now. Enough is enough.

The good news is Big Labor is not representative of South Carolina - we have good people, and this is an isolated incident. This video no more represents the people of our state than union bosses represent our workers.

But we can't let these kind of things define our state - we have to fight back.

Will you stand with me by making a contribution of $250, $100, or even $50 now to show Big Labor that we will not stand for their bullying?

Thank you again for your continued support and prayers! My very best,

Nikki

P.S.- Make a donation of $50 today to help us stand against Liberal union attacks. Donate here!" [36]

––––––––––––––––

"[W]hat I've lived and what I know: Women don't care about contraception. They care about jobs and the economy and raising their families and all of those things." [40]

"While we care about contraception, let's be clear. All we're saying is we don't want government to mandate when we have to have it and when we don't. We want to be able to make that decision." [40]

"'May the God of hope fill you with all joy and peace as you trust in Him, so that you may overflow with hope by the Holy Spirit' Romans 15:13. This was sent to me by my Pastor earlier in the week and I wanted to share. Good morning!" [42]

"My parents are immigrants, they came here legally, they put in the time, they put in the money, they did what they were supposed to. It makes them mad when they see illegal immigrants come into this state. " [43]

"It's My Life . . . ..Bon Jovi. Great song!

'You better stand tall

When they're calling you out

Don't bend, don't break

Baby, don't back down'" [44]

"That is not appropriate in South Carolina. We will give all of our candidates respect, and we certainly expect our candidates to come in and give the people of South Carolina respect." Referring to a Donald Trump speech with extensive profanity in Las Vegas. [41]

"Veto Fact: We vetoed the Arts Commission, not the arts. This does not defund arts education. This does defund an agency where over 30% of the funding goes to administrative services. We would not donate to a charity with those stats. Taxpayers should decide which arts programs to fund, not legislators. Michael and I love the arts but I don't believe it is a core function of govt during these economic times." [45]

"Pres. Obama is now telling SC that we can't enforce our illegal immigration laws. I'm trying to govern a state and the President keeps getting in my way. I will continue to fight him every step of the way." [47]

"Senator Graham, Congressman Duncan, and I had a press conference this morning on pushing forward for off shore drilling off the coast of South Carolina. It will be no closer than 10 miles off our coast. 50% will go towards paying down federal debt, 37.5% will go towards revenues in our state (infrastructure), and at least 12% towards land conservation. Jobs, jobs, jobs with a balance for the environment." [46]

(Referring to the Republican candidates for president in 2012): "We have a great field of candidates. President Obama can't ask for a "redo". Mr. President, God bless you . . . we wish you well . . . but it's time for you to go." [48]

"We'll make the unions understand full well that they are not needed, not wanted and not welcome in the state of South Carolina." [49]

JOHN KASICH, GOVERNOR OF OHIO

Governor John Kasich was born in 1952 in McKees Rocks, Pennsylvania, where he also grew up. Kasich graduated from Ohio State University in 1974 with a degree in political science. Kasich was elected to the Ohio Senate in 1978. He also a served as a member of the United States House of Representatives, representing Ohio's 12th congressional district from 1983-2001, including a stint as the Chairman of the House Budget Committee. After Congress, Kasich hosted "Heartland with John Kasich" on the Fox News Channel and guest hosted "The O'Reilly Factor." Kasich served on the board of directors for several corporations until becoming the managing director for Lehman Brothers' investment banking division in Columbus in 2001. Kasich is the author of three books: *Courage is Contagious*; *Stand for Something: The Battle for America's Soul*; and *Every Other Monday*. He defeated incumbent Democratic Governor Ted Strickland with 49% of the vote in a four-way race in 2010. In a November 2011 referendum, by a 61-39% vote, Ohioans overturned a bill Kasich had championed which limited the collective bargaining rights of public employees. Governor Kasich and his wife Karen Waldbillig have two children.

"I had this idiot pull me over on 315. Listen to this story. He says to me, he say, uh, he says you passed this emergency vehicle on the side of the road and you didn't yield. I said, officer I, are you kidding, I didn't, I didn't see any, I didn't even see any, where the heck was it?" He says, 'Well I understand that. Give me your license'. He goes back to the car, comes back, gives me a ticket and says you must report to court, if you don't report to court we're putting a warrant out for your arrest. He's an idiot!" [1]

"Save me from a cap and trade bill that's going to put a dagger in the Midwest and is basically one politician against slapping another on the back." [2]

"You know, Ohio is a great place. And it's - frankly, I'm a little taken aback at moments like this, but, frankly, I think I was put here for a good reason. And I thank the Lord for the blessings that he's given me throughout my lifetime, and I thank the Lord for the members of this General Assembly." [3]

"Look, we don't just have a fiscal crisis here. We have a jobs crisis in Ohio. The problem is we are not competitive. And if we can't control our costs and reduce our taxes and be able to be in a position to reduce our regulations the jobs are going to continue to leave. And when the jobs leave our families are hurt, our communities are hurt." [4]

"It's all in the pursuit of selfish power." Criticizing a liberal group that opposed his plan to privatize more state functions. [5]

"Now my concern with the teachers union is that I am convinced they are a lot more concerned with their own situation rather than the situation of our children. We need more school choice, we need to break the back of organized labor in the schools, and we need to turn our schools into institutions that excite our kids and teach them, and the best way to get it done is to give mothers and fathers the power to take their kids out of bad places and put them in good." [6]

"Young people, you know, our kids and our grandkids are leaving this state for better opportunities. One-third of Ohio college graduates are leaving this state within three years of graduating. Our best and our brightest, our seed corn, have decided that they need to go somewhere else to realize their hopes and dreams." [3]

"This is about kids. We cannot blow this opportunity . . . I said [to my congregation], 'There are 50 things I could ask you to pray for, but I ask you to pray for the Cleveland [school reform] plan.'" [7]

"When adults fight, children get lost in the shuffle . . . In this case, everybody got together and demanded that children be placed first." Discussing a reform plan for the Cleveland schools. [8]

"What we find is, when people don't have work, when they become hopeless, they turn to things they otherwise wouldn't turn to." Explaining why he believes that one reason to emphasize job creation is that it prevents drug abuse. [10]

"We live in a culture where every kid gets a trophy regardless of whether they kick it in to the goal or not. And then the kid goes out and gets a job, and then he goes home and says, 'Mom, I thought I was an A, and the supervisor keeps yelling at me and says I'm not any good.' There [needs to be] a balance." Calling for an overhaul of educational approaches working toward preparing more students to attend college. [9]

"Republicans and Democrats have long favored sentencing reform. Oh, we didn't get to this because we were afraid also. Forty-seven percent of our inmates sit in our state prisons for less than a year and they sometimes sit next to hardened criminals. It raises the recidivism rate, costs taxpayers a fortune. Again, to everyone who's here, 47 percent of people are in that prison for less than a year and we're sticking them in there next to somebody who's been a hardened criminal, a murderer, or God knows what else. And then they get out and their lives in too many cases are ruined. It doesn't even make any sense. And the reason we haven't changed it is because of fear." [3]

"Ohio has been under siege and not just from India and China. And, oh, yes, we live in a global world, and they're looking every day to take our simple products and move them overseas. And I want all of you to know that I have told one Chinese delegation after another that we don't like the fact that you manipulate your currency, we do not like the fact that you don't play on a level playing field when you trade with us, and it will stop. And we will be a strong voice in Ohio to make sure we get our fair share, India and China - they have us under." [3]

"But, you know, we're also under siege from Indiana, Kentucky, Georgia. Those from Dayton, NCR, gone. An empty building. We're under siege from North Carolina, from Florida, from Texas. They all come inside the boundaries of Ohio and they try to lure away our best and brightest. They take our jobs, sometimes they take our job creators out of our beloved Buckeye State. We're not going to let that continue. We cannot afford to let that continue." [3]

"In the last ten years, we lost 600,000 jobs. Only two states in America lost more: California, which is filled with whackadoodles, and Michigan which has got this . . . tremendous challenge with, uh, automobiles . . . lost more jobs than we did . . . That is not the Ohio that I know and it is not the Ohio that I found when I came here to go to Ohio State in 1970, which to me, was the promised land. This was the place where it was all happening. This was the place of the clean start. This was the place of the opportunity." [11]

"Many of you here today have been hungry to do something. Let us not let this opportunity pass to strengthen Ohio in this 21st Century. The enemy in Ohio right now is joblessness. The enemy in Ohio right now is poverty. And it is up to all of us to work together to defeat that enemy. Are you ready to defeat poverty and homelessness in Ohio?" [3]

"You think about the Cleveland Clinic, you think about University Hospital and Case Western Reserve, if you can't score a touchdown with those three assets, you are a knucklehead. We've got a lot of good things going for us. We have not been able to leverage those assets." Criticizing the Strickland Administration for the level of economic development in Cleveland. [12]

"Too many of our successful entrepreneurs flee the state to escape high taxation. And what I would say to all of you, Republicans and Democrats alike, you talk to those folks that have moved to Naples and you ask them why they have left. And they will tell you because they get a better deal. They get to keep more of what they have earned in their lifetime. And when they leave, we lose their money . . . " [3]

"If we can kill the death tax, maybe we can keep those people in Ashtabula County, and this whole region. If we keep them here, they are likely to create more jobs, they are likely to be creative, more innovative. All we care about is jobs, isn't it? We don't want to drive those people out." [6]

"We should be prepared to do more with less . . . for years. We need to seriously talk about what some of our options are going forward." [13]

"It was great to work with Republican and Democratic colleagues, including Ralph Nader, who sang a little song in my office to fight corporate welfare . . . So with corporate welfare, we're on it, okay?" [3]

"We promised Ohioans a new way and a new day, and we're delivering . . . This is the one they said couldn't be done." Signing a new Ohio budget in his office, June 29, 2011. [14]

"I can remember during the campaign going to Ashtabula County and having a young girl walk up to me and say, Mister, please don't tax my eggs. I go door to door and this is how I make a living. Please, Mister, don't break my business. You don't forget that." [3]

"There's a tremendous amount of change. I would argue this bill is the most comprehensive piece of legislation Ohio has passed in modern times .

. . Budgets are awfully boring things until you take a look at what we've done." [14]

"I don't support a 39 mph train, OK? It's not going to happen if I'm governor, OK? If you want the train, I hope you can get over that and vote for me anyway. But you're not going to get that train. It's a white elephant, we can't afford it, we can't pay for it. And who's riding it?" Criticizing the 3C passenger train proposal. [12]

"We're not going to run some program that some train cult wants to support." Criticizing the 3C passenger train proposal. [15]

"We'll have a series of options, but everybody needs to know: I'm not going away and I'm not going to take no for an answer here. The taxpayers deserve better than that, and we'll get there." On his support for his plan to raise taxes on fracking and cut income taxes. [16]

"This isn't popular to always say, but I believe there is a problem with climates, climate change in the atmosphere. I believe it. I don't know how much there is, but I also know the good Lord wants us to be good stewards of his creation. And so, at the end of the day, if we can find these breakthroughs to help us have a cleaner environment, I'm all for it." [17]

"Deval Patrick has done, in some ways, more radical things than I've done in Ohio." Praising Democratic Governor of Massachusetts Deval Patrick for enacting limits on collective bargaining. [18]

"These are change agents. Just because they worked somewhere where they might have been stifled. There was this guy one time, his name was Saul and he was on this road one time in Damascus and he became Paul. Just amazing isn't it? So, I'm very comfortable. I love our team. We are building a team of people that can plug together because that's what we need. No person can lift things. It takes a team." Responding to allegations that his administration lacked diversity and fresh faces." [19]

"It was the grace of the Lord empowering him to do what he did to change the face of our country. He not only touched the hearts and the souls of African-Americans, he touched the soul of white folks who lived in the suburbs and said, 'This is not the America that I love' . . . [My message to is], deep in your soul, you can figure out your purpose. As an African-American, you still have obstacles that are unique, in my opinion, to your race. Why not admit there are some people in our society that you have to go the extra mile for? I don't like that, I don't look at it that way, but it happens in our society. But you know what, when you are of excellence,

46

when you produce, when you know what you're doing - oh, they can deny you a few times, but they can't deny you forever." At a speech on Martin Luther King Jr., at historically black Central State University. [20]

––––––––––––––

"You know, it's a great story. I got a call from The Terminator. Arnold said, you need to meet this man, he's out there, he's meeting with every big official all over the world, he's got a program to do debt relief in Africa. And I'd always felt that foreign aid was a little bit of corporate welfare, but I always thought it could be applied well so that if we actually did immunize somebody or vaccinate them in another part of the world when extremists were shouting and criticizing America, the woman there would stand up and say, you may not like them, but they vaccinated my kid. See, I like that idea.

Arnold said, you've got to meet this guy. I said, what's his name? He said, you never heard of him. I said, what's his name, Arnold? He says, you've never heard of him. I said, what's his name? He said, his name is Bono. I said, Arnold, I'm not an Austrian bricklayer, I know who Bono is. So Bono and I sat down, and he talked about his faith. The song "I Still Haven't Found What I'm Looking For" is not about something he misplaced . . .

Bono says, you're not getting me in to see enough congressmen and senators. I said - this was in the early days - I said, Bono, look, you're wearing a black leather suit, Prada shoes, and those crazy sunglasses, they don't want to be seen with you. He said, John, the guys in my band, they don't want me to be seen with you."[3]

––––––––––––––

"I don't know that I can think of a greater evil. We knew that this existed in the world . . . and yet right under our nose is a lack of recognition of this problem - until Teresa [Fedor] wouldn't be quiet." Signing an executive order creating a task force to develop a plan to combat human trafficking in Ohio. [21]

"We're standing up and we're fighting. We're engaging in this war. So whether it is the judiciary, the prosecutors, the highway patrol, or whether it is those people who want to help these people recover their lives. 'Cause they can." Speaking in Toledo after signing a bill to combat human trafficking and provide services to victims. [22]

"Now everyone wants to say how partisan everything is. Baloney. That's not true. Oh, yeah, it's been partisan at times. Sometimes really partisan. I get it. I didn't fall off of a turnip truck over here." [24]

"Life is a gift from God and one way that we express our ongoing gratitude for it is by respecting it. This bill does that in a very fundamental way and I'm proud to have signed it into law." Statement on signing a bill banning abortions unless a physician determines the fetus could not be viable outside the womb. [23]

"We're alive again. We're out of the ditch. We're growing. It's happening in our state. It's not me. It's all of us and the people of this state. I'm just thrilled to be part of it. So it's happening, but we've got some cultural changes that we've got to make and people who represent the status quo are going to fight us on the next series of things we have to get done." [24]

"Glad that Ohio will be able to cast a vote against Obamacare this fall!" [25]

But, you know, I always worked in a bipartisan way when I was a United States Congressman. Ron Dellums, liberal Democrat, Oakland, California, I love Ron Dellums, one of my great friends. You know, I went to his wedding in California. I sat at a table with Willie Brown, Barbara Boxer, Dianne Feinstein. And I was the only Republican in San Francisco that day. But Dellums is coming here. He and I worked together, two lonely guys, trying to limit the production of the B-2 bomber. People thought we were - well, first of all, they called us the odd couple. A lot more, obviously, handsome than I am, and a brilliant man. Yeah, the Pentagon wanted 132. We ended up reaching agreement on 20 and saved a billion dollars a copy, and we built a team of Republicans and Democrats that limited the production of a major weapons system. I am told it never happened before in the 20th Century. [3]

"I'm the party line now, you know? I've never been uncomfortable with traveling a lonely road. I think that's what leaders do." Discussing calling for a tax on oil and gas drillers opposed by some of his party's legislative leaders. [26]

"I just want Ohio to be great; this is our chance. Please leave the cynicism and the political maneuvering at the door. Because we need you on the bus, and if you're not on the bus, we will run over you with the bus. And I'm not kidding. " [27]

For those who are sitting in this room that think, 'We've heard this before,' I had 12 visits by a president, somewhere between $45 (million) and $50 million [spent against me], 500 paid volunteers in here calling me every name in the book, former presidents, first ladies and God-knows-who-else, and we beat all of them. And if you think you're going to stop us, you're crazy. You will not stop us. We will beat you. And that's not arrogance." [27]

"We're alive again. We're out of the ditch. We're growing. It's happening in our state. It's not me. It's all of us and the people of this state." [36]

On passing a number of bills with bipartisan backing: "Public will never quite get it. You see it. It's amazing. I mean to put the politics in last place and put the public in first place, it's astounding." [28]

"Common sense has kind of gone out the window, and I know you're all going to hit me on that at some point." [34]

"[A severance tax on fracking is] going to happen. It's just a matter of when and what it's going to look like. I've had a number of offline conversations with industry. They understand this has to happen . . . Sometimes you have to give them space. I do push hard . . . but once in a while, they will call me up and say 'hey, hey, hey, hey, could you just give us some time on this?'" On his proposal for a severance tax on oil companies practicing fracking. [28]

"One year ago, I said we need to have a memorial. One year later, we are going to have a memorial on the grounds of this Statehouse. It will be the first memorial recognizing man's inhumanity to man in the United States of America [on the grounds of a state Capitol]." On his support for a memorial to victims of the Holocaust and to the troops from Ohio who helped to liberate Nazi death camps. [33]

"We never thought [former Cleveland Browns quarterback] Bernie Kosar would bring the Browns back and win that big championship game." Commenting on how he thought his side could prevail with an upset win in a statewide vote on collective bargaining the next week, not realizing that Kosar lost all three AFC title games in which he played. [30]

"They talk about this problem with binding arbitration. It doesn't make a lot of sense to me to have somebody from Los Angeles fly into Zanesville and impose a wage settlement on you . . . and then they're on the plane back to Los Angeles." [31]

"I'm not singing in any chorus for LeBron James . . . Look, he's a great basketball player, he's a great guy. There's a lot of great people in Ohio . . . We've lost 400,000 jobs out here and the last guy I worry about is LeBron James. You know I mean, we all hope he'll stay in Cleveland. We think we've got a great guy there that can turn everything around, but we got some serious problems." Saying that unlike the incumbent governor, Ted Strickland, he would not be willing to appear in a music video designed to persuade Cleveland Cavaliers basketball star (and Akron native) LeBron James to re-sign with Cleveland. James wound up accepting a free agent offer from the Miami Heat. [32]

"We have so many stupid rules and regulations that prevent us from getting the best people to come in here. You just can't believe it. Now I blame it on all of you [reporters], all this transparency and conflicts and all this other stuff, I just want to tell you, it is a problem to get quality people to come to work in the government. Our problems in government are bigger and the quality of people who want to come in is less. Now, if you get sick and your disease gets worse and worse and worse, I would suggest to you [that] you get a better and better doctor. But today if you get sick under the governmental rules and all the political correctness and open sunshine and all this other stuff, you get a worse doctor. This is something we have to think about over time." [34]

Predicting the 2012 Ohio presidential race: "Oh, it's going to be close. It will be, you know, tight as a tick out here, David. It always is." [35]

"I don't read newspapers in the state of Ohio. Very rarely do I read a newspaper. Because . . . reading newspapers does not give you an uplifting experience . . . I have found my life is a lot better if I don't get aggravated by what I read in the newspaper." [29]

"Over the years people drink more. It's just a natural revenue stream." Discussing a plan to lease the state's liquor distribution system. [37]

"I find myself tripping over the anthills on the way to the pyramids." [34]

On whether he had a backup plan in case voters repealed his law limiting collective bargaining: "I never think ahead." [38]

"We're the best darned fair in the entire country! . . . This is a chance to show people that bread doesn't just show up in a grocery store. Agriculture is the bedrock of this fair." Speaking at the opening of the 2011 Ohio State Fair, Wednesday, July 27, 2011. [39]

PAUL LEPAGE, GOVERNOR OF MAINE

Governor Paul LePage was born in Lewiston, Maine in 1948 and was one of eighteen children in a poor, French-speaking home. At age eleven, after being beaten by his father, he ran away from home and was homeless for several years. LePage was helped by Peter Snowe, the first husband of Senator Olympia Snowe, to gain admission to college. LePage graduated from Husson College (now University) with a degree in business administration and earn edhis M.B.A. from the University of Maine. LePage worked for a lumber company in Canada, founded consulting firm LePage & Kasevich Inc., and in 1996, was hired as general manager of Marden's, a major Maine discount retailer. LePage was mayor of Waterville from 2003-2011. He was elected in a five-way race with 38% of the vote in 2010, becoming the first Franco-American elected as Governor of Maine. A 2011 law he signed that would have ended Election Day voter registration was overturned by voters by a 60-40% vote. Governor LePage and his wife Ann have three children.

"I absolutely believe that the federal government should put people before eagles. We've gotten to a point in our society where people don't count. People pay taxes, eagles don't." In response to a question about moving an eagle's nest from a roadway. [1]

Paul LePage: "I'm about ready to punch [reporter] A.J. Higgins."

Reporter Jennifer Rooks: "Don't punch him."

Paul LePage: "Oh, come on."

Jennifer Rooks: "No, no."

Candidate LePage expressing his desire to punch reporter A. J. Higgins after Higgins has asked him tough questions at an Augusta press conference. (LePage later said he was joking: "I'm like a dog. I bark more than I bite and I've never bitten anyone yet.") [2]

"There was an editorial that says, you can take the person off the streets but you can't take the street out of the person, and I will readily admit that if you are on your own from 11 years old on there's a little bit of that that stays; that as much as you try, some of that stays." Discussing his bluntness. [2]

"We came from behind because we have a message. We have a message that says: One, we've had enough of the federal government. We've had enough. Two, we've had enough of the state government. And No. 3, government should be working for the people, not the people working for the government . . . And as your governor, you're gonna be seeing a lot of me on the front page saying 'Gov. LePage tells Obama to go to hell.'" [3]

"Quite frankly, the science that I'm looking at says there is no [problem]. There hasn't been any science that identifies that there is a problem. The only thing that I've heard is if you take a plastic bottle and put it in the microwave and you heat it up, it gives off a chemical similar to estrogen. So the worst case is some women may have little beards." [4] On proposals to ban the chemical, BPA.

"[The NAACP] are a special interest. End of story. And I'm not going to be held hostage by special interests. Tell 'em to kiss my butt." [5]

"I went to work at 11 years old. I became governor. It's not a big deal. Work doesn't hurt anybody." [6]

"We could have entertainment, festivals, but nobody wants to come to Maine because if they're here more than 10 days, you've got to pay income tax in Maine." [7]

"Now that I'm governor of Maine, there's nothing left to steal." Speaking at the Franco-American Heritage Center [formerly St. Mary's Catholic Church] in Lewiston, Maine, March 16, 2011. LePage told the crowd that when he was twelve, he stole Halloween candy from children, and used the story as a way of discussing the state's finances. [8]

"I was born here, I was baptized here, I made my first confession here. And I spent more time in there." [Pointing toward the confessional] [8].

"I don't know if you know this, but the State of Maine is the only state in the United States of America that charges sales tax on bull semen. You hear that? Bull semen." [9] This was not true.

"My answer stands. I will feed Maine people before I feed foreigners." Responding to a question asking why he was cutting welfare payments to legal non-citizen residents. [10]

"In the state of Maine, in the last two weeks, we had two children in the morgue, two mothers in the morgue, and two fathers who blew their brains out. The problem in the state of Maine is the laws are too lenient. I tried to make changes and the Legislature didn't want to make them." [10]

"And the state of Maine made me do a three-month buffalo study," Did you hear what I said? Buffalo study. The next spring, they decided that they still didn't want this project to be built so they had us go out and count black flies, two months counting black flies. That tells me that the attitude of the regulatory agency was very adversarial to that project." [11] Regulators denied the accuracy of this statement.

"[Windmills] are doing an awful lot of damage to our quality of life, our mountains. I don't think it's going to lower the cost of energy. I think in 10 years we're going to be like Sweden and Denmark and we're going to be swearing at ourselves." [12]

"And it's non-partisan and that's a problem, because it's gridlock. Everybody is divided and we can't get anything done." On why he decided not to go to the National Governor's Association 2011 summer meeting. [13]

"LURC, like the Department of Environmental Protection and the Environmental Protection Agency, have become control freaks. The state of Maine needs regulatory oversight, not regulatory control." Regarding the Land Use Regulation Commission, which oversees 10.4 million acres of unorganized territory in northern Maine. [14]

"In southern Maine, yes, there's a lot of kooks down there." LePage's response to another Republican gubernatorial candidate who said the Legislature should be reduced by one-third because there would be fewer lawmakers from Portland who "hatch and promote kooky ideas in this state." [14]

"I don't care where you go in this country. If you come from Maine you're looked down upon. Twenty years ago if you came from Maine, they couldn't wait to get you into their school." [15] At a press conference promoting a set of education policies.

"We should have exempted them, and if they get in trouble, they can call the pope." On a Maine regulation that requires everyone - including nuns - to purchase heath insurance with maternity coverage. [16]

"'I would love to tax the rich if we had any in Maine." Response to a suggestion to "tax the rich" to balance the state budget. [17]

"It breaks my heart to see an old lady . . . she has to choose between food, medicine or oil. If it were up to me, I'd find a dungeon very cheaply and house them all." Response to a question about the possibility of privatizing prisons. [17]

"The Earth was a lot warmer in the year 1100. So I don't know. Are there signs of it? Yes." Response to a question about whether he believed in global warming. [17].

"I'm working for the people of Maine, not the whales of Maine." [18]

"Too many of our kids are leaving the state. We have to stop that exodus. We have to convince the federal government that we're not hurting our resource, we're sustaining it." [18]

"Anybody [who] tells you any different is blowing smoke. We as a state will not prosper until the private sector prospers." On the need to reduce regulations on Maine's natural resources-based businesses." [18]

"Buying a Maine daily newspaper is like paying someone to lie to you. Frankly folks, until they get more objective, they're going to get as much wrath from me as they give me." [18]

"It was a dysfunctional family and my dad and I didn't see eye to eye and he beat me, and I left. End of story . . . Sometimes I'd stay at friend's homes, sometimes I'd stay in hallways. I've stayed in cars, cellars, the racetrack . . . It's always a matter of just finding a place to live, and getting jobs. You work and you've got money and as long as you've got money, a place to live and clothes, I just never really thought about it, I just did it. You were there and you just make it work." [19]

"There was no such thing back then, there was no homeless shelters. You'd just have to make do and you just roamed around and you figured it out." [19]

"Shelters are very, very important for a very short period of time." [19]

"We can stop homelessness to a great extent if we catch it early. We need to figure out a way to catch it early. A lot of people have exhausted their savings. They've exhausted their ability to pay their mortgage, their car payments, student loans and unfortunately they're the forgotten few because what happens here in the state if you own any assets you don't qualify for any help. Well, they have to lose it all before we'll help them and that's a gap we need to figure out." [19]

"If it is to be, it is up to me. Those are the most powerful ten words and if you really get to understand them there's nothing you can't do if you want to. It's all about putting your mind to it and staying to course." [19]

"Husson faculty made a difference in my life. As you may know in a story reported last year, I had a challenging childhood. I also had difficulty - some would say I still have it - because my first language was and is French." Speech at Husson University in Bangor upon receiving an honorary doctorate. [20]

"Some of those strippers were like surrogate moms." On some who helped LePage when he was homeless between the ages of eleven and thirteen. [21]

"Companies have told me, show us that you are moving in a different direction and excite us and we'll look at Maine . . . In four years if people think I failed, they'll send me into retirement." [21]

"As many of you know, I left home at the age of 11 with nowhere to go. But being homeless was the better alternative of being abused. I understand how domestic abuse can tear a family apart and I am aware of the sensitivity of the issue. I have zero tolerance for domestic abuse. There is no reason to inflict this abuse on anyone ever." [22]

"Back then, it was hand-to-mouth, week-to-week." "We had to build an organization and it was hard work . . . Now, it's time to make it a real shelter. The building they've had all these years was held together with Band-Aids and wood glue . . . [L]ook deep and hard into the mission of the shelter and dig deep into your pockets." Speaking at a fundraising launch event for a shelter in Waterville, Maine. [23]

"Believe me, it is a challenge when you're 11 years old on the streets homeless, sleeping in cellars, sleeping in hallways, sleeping with friends." Speaking to students at Learning Works in Portland, which serves at-risk, immigrant and low-income youth. [24]

"On occasion, when they've treated me in a way I didn't like, I treated them [the same way] back." At Learning Works, after saying [with the exception of the press] students should treat others as they want to be treated. [24]

"Go down the right road, instead of the left one." At Learning Works in Portland. LePage then pointedly looked at former Democratic state senator Ethan Strimling, the group's CEO. [24]

"On August 6, I encourage us also to all pray for our troops who tirelessly fight in the defense of our country . . . Family and our freedoms should never be taken for granted. We are a nation that has hit a troubling era and praying for the strength to do what is right for our people is the right thing to do." From weekly radio address. [27]

"We've been saying it for two years now that you can't spend what you don't have and it's coming to roost . . . We'll see as we go along, If you get to $25 [million] and there is still room and you get $50 [million] and there is still room and, if at $75 [million] it hurts, you stop. But if $100 [million] still seems easy, you go to $125 [million]. You go until it hurts . . . It's just like a business. You get all the necessities done and you make sure the services are provided and you stop then." [28]

"It's all a big play and I think it's bullshit." [Then pausing for a minute] "Bull. Shit." After meeting with a group of unemployed workers who had demanded a meeting. [29]

———————————

Governor LePage: "The press, you folks ran out and wrote all these articles and you never once called us and checked."

Reporter Keith Baldi: "I actually talked to [acting press secretary] Adam Fisher. I talked to Adam Fisher and he was in my story."

LePage: "How would Adam Fisher know? He was never in my office for the meeting, he was never in my office."

Baldi: "He was the spokesperson that day."

LePage (to reporters): "You, sir, have been very honest and very fair, and I apologize. So have you, Don. Most of you in media have been very well. But, those who write, except Mal Leary, those who write in print, have been totally dishonest, totally unwilling to do your jobs, and you spend too much time on the blogs."

After the abrupt resignation of Department of Marine Resources Commissioner Norm Olsen who sent a letter to media outlets describing disagreements with the LePage administration. [25]

———————————

"It's clear now, Congress and the White House antics over raising the nation's $14.3 trillion borrowing limit has cost Americans . . . The U.S credit rating downgrade from AAA to AA+ will deeply affect our nation in a way that we have not experienced since 1917 . . . Using debt default as a bargaining chip rather than putting our fiscal house back in order was an enormously risky maneuver that failed. It is a major setback for our future and economic credibility of our country and it's time our leaders in Washington start working to get our economy back on track instead of worrying about upcoming elections." [26]

"The Francos were sort of the slaves of the north and back in 1922, there was a massive KKK rally against the French coming down from Canada and so, yeah, it has a very very special meeting to most of the Francos here in Maine." Speaking at Martin Luther King, Jr. Day Breakfast in Waterville, Maine, January 16, 2012. [30]

"I don't know what planet you're on . . . It would be hell freezes over before you would ever support a Republican." Responding to former Democratic state senator Judy Paradis' criticism of his proposed Medicaid cuts at a workshop in Fort Kent, Maine, December 27, 2011. [34]

"Am I one hundred percent in favor of the [state Republican party] platform? I'm not 100 percent in favor of anything. It's a working document, like the Constitution is a working document. The Bible is a working document. There's always something that can be enhanced or changed." [31]

"I would rather put my foot in my mouth than have [Democratic gubernatorial nominee] Libby Mitchell with her hands in your pockets." [32]

"I got an e-mail [recently] that said, 'He who dare not offend cannot speak the truth.' Let me tell you what's important about that quote. Our society and the press does not, does not want to hear the truth. What they want is political correctness. And I don't blame them, because what I said the other day was pretty off the mark, and I deserved to get kicked in the butt for it. And it did hurt us a little bit in the polls, but it didn't hurt us anywhere near what you've heard . . . But I appreciate the press for attacking me, because I do need to get a little bit smarter." [32]

"I'm a good actor, I'll leave it at that . . . I know how to push hard . . . I pushed hard, and I'll push even harder this time [in my second year in office]." Interview with WCSH-TV's Don Carrigan. [33]

"That's coming from a little spoiled brat from Portland. He's very fortunate that his granddad was born ahead of him." Referring to State Senator Justin Alfond (D-Portland)'s criticism of Department of Health and Human Services Secretary Mary Mayhew. Afond's grandfather was a businessman and philanthropist. [34]

"We wanted to introduce choice so that parents of children could decide where they want their children to go to school . . . What our four [educational] bills try to do is ask 'What is best for the student?'" [34]

"One [school] superintendent per county is all this state needs." [34]

"When I went to the unions I said 'The reason we have a problem is that you are protecting bad teachers and you do absolutely nothing for good teachers.'" [34]

"I've been called a bully, I've been called everything. I go on vacation to give them a break and they complain about that. It's really tough being governor. Not only do you have to listen to 'em all the time, you have to sit in oversight of the largest adult day care in the state of Maine." [39]. Talking about going on vacation while the Maine Legislature was working on the state budget.

'Unfortunately in state government there's three kinds of jobs. There's an appointed job, which I have control over, these people up here from the standpoint they work for me; we have protected jobs or civil servant jobs, which is one step better than being in the union but we still have very limited control over; and then you have the state union." Comments at town hall meeting in Newport, Maine. [35]

"Believe me, there is a lot of good and hard working people that work for the state. They are not the problem. The problem is the middle management of the state is about as corrupt as you can be. Believe me we're trying every day to get them to go to work, but it's hard." [35]

"Dear State Employees,

. . . When my Administration came into office, we promised Maine people we would not settle for the status quo . . .

I hear every day how much more customer-friendly the State has become. However, for whatever reason, some employees have not come on board. Roadblocks have put up, hurdles have been thrown in the way, and information has not been passed up to senior management. Those employees want to keep doing the same thing because it was always been done that way. Quite frankly, that attitude is unacceptable. In my opinion, it shows they have been corrupted by the bureaucracy.

When the union bosses tell employees they should not participate in the Administration's initiatives and instead just "ride it out," we are dealing with a lack of integrity. In other words we are dealing with corruption.

If you are working hard for the people of Maine and following the leadership of your Commissioners, then keep up the good work - you know who you are. If you are dragging your feet because you do not like the direction the Administration is headed, then it time to either get on board or get out of the way." From a letter to state employees, April 27, 2012. [36]

"In the state of Maine that is exactly what we are trying to do, to go down to a 4 percent flat tax with no exemptions for anyone. The problem I see is this: Until we as Americans decide whether we want to continue down the path of a welfare entitlement country, or we want to revive the American dream, we are not going to get there." [38]

"Well, let me tell you this. I came from the streets. I was a runaway kid at 11 and I was on the streets. And I went to a parochial school. And the reason it was good for me is I needed enormous discipline when I was a kid. We don't have that in public schools. So if faith-based schools have a different approach to teaching and it worked for me-so, I believe there might be some other kids out there like me that need a good education, and it's probably going to come from the faith-based. It wasn't the religious part of it that was good. It was the brothers being stern-and look at my knuckles! They still show I was hit a few times." [37]

"Despite the fact that we have a Republican governor, a Republican House and a Republican Senate, let me tell you this, in the House and the Senate, a lot of people say they are something they are really not." [39]

"The press makes us out to be the big bad guy. But we care about people and families. Today is important. It's important we get together to care about life." [40]

"My pledge to Maine people is very simple: It's going to be people ahead of politics . . . The word 'people' appears in the Maine Constitution 49 times. You cannot find a single mention of the words 'politics,' 'Republican,' 'Democrat,' 'Green,' or 'Independent' in 37 pages of preambles, articles and sections of our Constitution. The framers had it right." At his swearing in ceremony, January 6, 2011. [41]

"Nothing, haven't done a damn thing. The Legislature hasn't passed anything worthwhile." [42]

"In the last 60 days I've been relegated to selling newspapers. Why? Because we have nothing to do until legislators in Augusta, both Democrats and Republicans, do their job." [43]

"I went on vacation last week because I had nothing to do. Because I'm waiting. I'm waiting for legislation. I cannot do anything until the Legislature acts. And we need action." [43]

"That building is not an organized labor building. End of story." "It's the Department of Labor, not the Department of Organized Labor and until we make that determination it needs to be neutral. That's where my position is, it's a neutral position." Regarding the removal of a mural about labor history. [44]

"I'd laugh at them, the idiots. That's what I would do. Come on! Get over yourselves!" Response to a question about what he would do if mural supporters formed a human chain to prevent its removal. [45]

"It's all about getting back on topic." "I told them that it's time that both the House and the Senate and the administration focus on the task at hand, and that's pension reform, health care reform, regulatory reform, energy reform and lowering the tax on Maine people." On what he told Senate Republicans in a private meeting held after some wrote him a letter criticizing his rhetoric. [46]

"Zipping my mouth and not offending them." Explaining to reporters what he discussed with Maine Senate Republicans in a closed meeting. [46]

"Dear Representative Pingree: I was disappointed to see your recent letter to Secretary Sebelius. It appears that you have become part of the jet-setting Washington culture that keeps people dependent on government handouts. Your efforts should instead be focused on the Maine people, helping my administration create the well-paying careers that will let Mainers earn their own way and create prosperity for themselves." [47]

"This November represents a real choice at the ballot box. Do you want to remain a sinking welfare state? Maine's welfare program is cannibalizing the rest of state government . . . To all you able-bodied people out there: Get off the couch and get yourself a job. I understand welfare because I lived it. I understand the difference between a want and a need. The Republican Party promised to bring welfare change. We must deliver on this promise." [48]

'Before the media coronates him, let me do it. Angus King is the king of the wind cartel. Yes, he's likeable, but let's not forget that he has made a fortune off your backs." [48]

"One of you sitting out there may be standing up here in a few years . . . We are working to bring prosperity to this great state and we are doing it for all of you. We want you to make Maine your lifelong home. We want you to become the job leaders of tomorrow. Help us by giving us your talents . . . to dream big . . . We need to look forward and stop looking at the past. The state of Maine is making progress, more progress than some would have you believe. I ask you new graduates to join me in that fight . . . You can, you can, yes, you can." Commencement address at Thomas College, 2012. [49]

"Domestic violence is a very serious problem in society. I'm trying to encourage you to do two things: If you've never been exposed to it, please don't. Secondly, if you have been, you need to help me stop it. Because too many people are getting hurt and too many people are dying." Speaking to students at a job training program [50]

"There's nothing in the world you can't do if you put your mind to it. It's that simple. You don't have to be a rocket scientist. Believe me, I'm not the brightest guy on earth." [50]

"Me be president? The country couldn't stand it." [50]

"Last week it was reported that Maine was one of just six states last year to experience a decline in the size of its economy-measured by Gross Domestic Product, or GDP. Maine was the only state in New England with a decline in 2011. Taken in isolation, that statistic sounds like we have not been working on solutions. Indeed, politicians and liberal bloggers have used it to advocate against my administration's policies. They have also tried to say that borrowing more money will bring back our economy. However, Washington tried stimulus; it failed to produce results and has increased the massive debt the federal government is leaving for our grandchildren." [51]

"Washington DC now has the power to dictate how we, as Americans, live our lives. This is a massive overreach by the federal government, and is infringing upon the individual choices that we, as Americans, have in pursuing our own American Dream.

"This decision has verified what President Obama has refused to admit all along, which is to say this law is an enormous tax on the American people. The federal government can force you to do or buy anything, as long as they call it a 'tax.' This massive tax hike will only destroy the American economy as it forces us over the financial cliff . . . This decision erodes the freedoms which made the United States the greatest country on Earth. It is a sad day, and it is now up to the American people to demand full repeal of Obamacare. The Washington DC elites cannot and should not run our lives." Statement reacting to the U. S. Supreme Court ruling holding that most of the Affordable Care Act is constitutional." [52]

"Democrats are attacking Republicans saying that we are turning down free health care. I have always said it doesn't matter if the money is taken from the left or right pocket, it's still my pocket. Make no mistake about it, taxpayers will pay for this." [53]

"This decision has made America less free. We the people have been told there is no choice. You must buy health insurance or pay the new Gestapo - the I.R.S." [53]

"It was not my intent to insult anyone, especially the Jewish Community, or minimize the fact that millions of people were murdered. Clearly, what has happened is that the use of the word Gestapo has clouded my message.

Obamacare is forcing the American people to buy health insurance or else pay a tax. Our health care system is moving toward one that rations care and negatively impact millions of Americans.

We are no longer are a free people. With every step that Obamacare moves forward, our individual freedoms are being stripped away by the Federal Government. This should anger all Americans." Press release on having compared the IRS to the Gestapo. [54]

––––––––––––––

Reporter Paul Merrill: "May I ask you about your comments from Saturday?"

Governor LePage: "No, you can't."

Merrill: "I just did."

LePage: "And I'm not gonna answer you."

Merrill: You're not gonna say anything? People are upset about . . ."

LePage: "Talk to this lady right here."

Merrill: "She said that you guys were not commenting today. Will you apologize?"

LePage: "To who?"

Merrill: "To the people who are upset."

LePage: "Well, who? Who's upset?"

Merrill: "The Anti Defamation League is upset. There's a group of, there's a group of Jewish people down in Southern Maine."

LePage: "It was never intended to offend anyone. And if someone's offended, then they ought to be goddamned mad at the Federal Government."

Merrill: "Is that an apology?"

Dialogue, on LePage having compared the IRS to the Gestapo [55]

––––––––––––––

"What I am trying to say is the Holocaust was a horrific crime against humanity and, frankly, I would never want to see that repeated. Maybe the IRS is not quite as bad - yet . . . They're headed in that direction . . . You know why? Rationing." Comments to Vermont reporter Paul Heintz on having compared the IRS to the Gestapo [56]

———————

Governor LePage: "You're not being what I call an objective reporter. You're being a blogger."

Reporter Paul Heintz: "What have I reported?"

LePage: "Well, your questions are clearly slanted."

Heintz: "My questions? I'm asking questions to you, I'm not reporting anything. I'll report something later on once I get back to my office and do that. You can read that and judge my work at that point."

LePage: "Do I think the IRS is intentionally going to kill someone? No. Do I think that the ACA is going to force rationing on the American people? Yes. And I don't know if you know what rationing means, but I would research Canada and see if they have put limits on medical care based on ages, based on diseases. That is the clear issue. OK?"

Dialogue with Vermont reporter on having compared the IRS to the Gestapo [57]

———————

"The acts of the Holocaust were nothing short of horrific. Millions of innocent people were murdered and I apologize for my insensitivity to the word and the offense some took to my comparison of the IRS and the Gestapo. However, I want to make this very clear; it was never my intent to insult or to be hurtful to anyone, but rather express what can happen by overreaching government. I fear we have a federal government that is moving toward a socialistic state and we must not forget history because if we do we are bound to repeat it." [58]

SUSANA MARTINEZ, GOVERNOR OF NEW MEXICO

Governor Susana Martinez was born in El Paso, Texas in 1959. Martinez is the first female governor of New Mexico as well as the first Latina governor in the United States. She graduated from the University of Texas at El Paso with a degree in criminal justice and later earned her law degree from the University of Oklahoma College of Law. Susana Martinez was an attorney for the New Mexico Children, Youth and Families Department, 1993 to 1996; assistant district attorney and deputy district attorney, 1986 to 1993. She was District Attorney for the Third Judicial District in Doña Ana County from 1996-2008, a position for which she was elected four times. Before running for District Attorney, Martinez switched her party registration to Republican. Martinez was elected Governor in 2010 with 54% of the vote. Governor Martinez and her husband Chuck Franco have one child.

"For too long, soft-on-crime politicians have focused less on the rights of victims and more on the rights of criminals. That will end in a Martinez Administration. I will make accountability the order of each and every day.

Criminals will be made to understand New Mexico is not a place they want to visit, much less reside in. I will be a strong advocate for tougher laws to protect the most vulnerable among us, including children, the disabled and seniors.

As a prosecutor, public safety has always been my top priority. As governor, I will fight to reinstate the death penalty for the most horrendous crimes. Those who murder law enforcement officials, witnesses and children in the course of a sexual assault should face the ultimate punishment." [1]

"I'm not sure the science completely supports [the idea that human activity is involved in global warming]." [2]

"If [illegal aliens] commit a crime, we should prosecute them and then deport them. Then the federal government has a bigger hammer [should the convicted criminal return.] [But Republicans ought to be] very much in favor of lawful immigration." [3]

"This order [to check the immigration status of people arrested for crimes] takes the handcuffs off of New Mexico's law enforcement officers in their mission to keep our communities safe. The criminal justice system should have the authority to determine the immigration status of all criminals, regardless of race or ethnicity, and report illegal immigrants who commit crimes to federal authorities."[4]

"I hope I've been able to show other young girls that as long as you work hard and you're committed to fight for your education, that anything's possible." [5]

"When I first registered to vote I registered as a Democrat. My parents were Democrats. I moved to Las Cruces, New Mexico in 1986 and again registered as a Democrat." "[But when two Republican friends took her and her husband out to lunch], we started to have a conversation about the issues. They never talked about 'Republican' or used the word 'conservative.' When we got back in the car I said to my husband, 'Oh my God, we're Republicans!'" [3]

"It's sort of like a wedding invitation, where you keep reminding people. " On encouraging other governors on both sides of the Mexican border to attend a meeting to be held in Albuquerque. [6]

"I know [my paternal grandparents] arrived without documents, especially my father's father." [7].

"Thanks to the expanded version of Katie's Law, which requires a DNA sample from anyone arrested for a felony, we have seen a remarkable rise in DNA matches that have allowed us to put more criminals behind bars . . . New Mexico now has one of the toughest versions of Katie's Law in the country, and it's working." [11]

"No, I won't be [running for vice-president] and this is why: the reason is I ran for governor. I gave a promise to the people of New Mexico that I would be the governor for the next four years. We have an agenda. We're going to make sure that we're going to take care of business. We have to do this right. I can't do this for a few months and then take on to another path."[9]

"Sixty-seven percent of Hispanic voters support the repeal of this law [allowing illegal immigrants to get New Mexico driver's licenses] . . . I think what's important is this isn't just about Hispanics. This is about people from all over the world coming to New Mexico with a sole purpose of getting a driver's license, a very valid and valuable ID, using false documentation, and then leaving our state. It's not that I'm Hispanic and that some of the folks coming here are Hispanic. It's about public safety . . . It becomes a United States ID and they go and trade it in another state, and that state never intended for an illegal immigrant to possess that kind of a license." [8]

"I'm pro-life, I have seen what abortion can do to a woman and when there isn't a lot of thought being given, when it's simple. I've seen women who see abortion as a method of contraception instead of the thoughtful process that it absolutely deserves without the other alternative being discussed. I do oppose partial birth abortion. I think that is atrocious, that child is partial birth, you are born and then you are killed, and that is atrocious. That is a late term abortion and I don't support that." [10]

"I have always maintained that immigration reform should take place at the federal level, and that is consistent with the Supreme Court ruling today. While I never supported an Arizona-style law in New Mexico, I understand the frustration felt by Arizonans, given the federal government's failure to address the immigration issue . . . In New Mexico, we have tackled public-safety issues relating to border security in responsible ways, such as ending the sanctuary state policy that prevented state police from checking the immigration status of those arrested for crimes, and seeking to repeal the law that gives driver's licenses to illegal immigrants." [12]

"Sometimes Republicans engage in number-crunching analysis that doesn't always take the neediest into account. We have to factor them in before we start proposing these cuts." [13]

"I absolutely advocate for comprehensive immigration reform. Republicans want to be tough and say, 'Illegals, you're gone.' But the answer is a lot more complex than that." [13]

"New Mexico's driver's license policy has once again attracted criminal elements to our state in pursuit of a government-issued identification card. Our current system jeopardizes the safety and security of all New Mexicans and it is abundantly clear that the only way to solve this problem is to repeal the law that gives driver's licenses to illegal immigrants." [14]

"I have to deliver the results I promised, because as the first Hispanic female governor, I'm going to pave a path of some kind. I want it to be one that little Hispanic girls will want to follow." [13]

"A horse's companionship is a way of life for many people across New Mexico. We rely on them for work and bond with them through their loyalty. I believe creating a horse-slaughter industry in New Mexico is wrong, and I am strongly opposed." [15]

"A parent, a guardian should know that the person who lives next door is a convicted [sexual] predator." On seeking to close a legal loophole that unintentionally thwarted registration of sex offenders. [16]

"My mother was responsible for everything. If something broke in the house, Mom would say, 'You can't wait for someone else to fix it. So we'll figure out how to fix it ourselves.'" [17]

BUTCH OTTER, GOVERNOR OF IDAHO

Governor "Butch" Otter was born in Caldwell, Idaho in 1942. After beginning to study for the priesthood in Washington state, Otter attended Boise Junior College (now Boise State University) and then the College of Idaho, from which he graduated with a B.A. in political science in 1967. He served in the Idaho Army National Guard from 1968 to 1973. Otter served in the Idaho House of Representatives from 1973-1976. He served as President of Simplot International, a large food and agribusiness company based in Idaho and worked for them for thirty years. He served as Lieutenant Governor of Idaho and then, beginning in 2001, served three terms in the U S. House. Otter, one of three Republicans to vote against the 2001 Patriot Act, said in 2011, "I thought it was a fundamental violation of the constitution. I still think so. In essence what the legislative branch did was give the executive branch license to search anywhere, tap anybody's phone, do anything they want." Otter was first elected governor in 2006 and re-elected in 2010 with 59% of the vote. Butch Otter married Lori Easley in 1996.

"I went all over the world. I got to deal with a lot of different countries. And when I would come home I would say, 'My biggest problem getting a project going in a foreign country is my own government.' It always was. With the exception of a couple of agencies, my biggest problem was the government saying, 'No, we don't want you to do this, no, we don't want you do that.'" On traveling on behalf of his employer, J.R. Simplot, a major potato company. [1]

"In the West, we have what is called a brand. That brand is yours; you put it on stuff that you own. And that flag is our brand, as Americans. Anyone who wants to burn that up-they can't defile my brand with their free speech." Speaking in favor of a Constitutional amendment to ban flag desecration while a member of Congress. [1]

"I still support medical marijuana. You go to some of these places where people have cancer. Some of these people, the only way they can get relief is by smoking marijuana. I was in favor of Oregon's right to die law. I wouldn't ever suggest that in Idaho, but that's what that state wanted." [1].

"No one has opposed Obamacare more vehemently than me . . . However, ending Obamacare by whatever means does not alleviate the need for Idaho to develop its own solutions to healthcare issues in our state."-Message vetoing a bill that would prevent Idaho from establishing a state health care insurance exchange. [2]

"News flash: Regularly eating ANYTHING in an irresponsible way contributes to weight gain and other health concerns!" Responding to a report that potatoes foster weight gain. [3]

"I'm prepared to bid for that first ticket to shoot a wolf myself." Speaking to a hunters rally after signing legislation to allow limited hunting of wolves and declaring wolves a state "disaster emergency." [4]

"I am thoroughly disappointed and frustrated with the [federal] court's decision today returning wolves to federal protection. Idaho has done everything asked of us by the federal government in order to delist wolves in our state and restore state management . . . The number of wolves in Idaho today is almost triple the population necessary for delisting throughout all three states. I don't know why any state would ever allow another reintroduction of a species because the federal government and radical environmentalists simply cannot live up to their word and allow state management." [5]

"Otter doesn't want to cut. I would like to see some compassion. This is a tough tough position to be in and I've got to pick and I've got to choose." [6]

"I don't like taking anybody's choices away from the . . . " Explaining his opposition to a proposal to close Idaho's open primaries [7]

When you're high on dope, you're not free . . . [On defense], I think you have got to be the toughest kid on the block in this world." In disagreeing with Ron Paul's positions on drugs and the military [14]

"I don't think it sends the wrong message." "The thing that irritates me I guess the most about the (U.S.) State Department's policy toward Cuba is that it's not a policy toward Cuba. You all sitting right here in this room, it's a policy against you. You're a free American, you oughta be able to travel anywhere you want, whenever you want." On plans for a trade mission to Cuba [7]

"This place moves a lot faster than Washington, D.C., but still not as fast as the private sector. Y'know, you can go to lunch and have a discussion over lunch and that can become your policy at 1 o'clock when you get back to the plant. You can't do that here. "A governor [needs more patience]-and that's not one of my long suits." [8]

On not holding any press conferences in his first six weeks as Governor: "Haven't had to - because I've been accessible. Anybody that wants to get in and talk to ya, or sometimes I run into folks out in the hallway or in the gym working out. Y'know, sometimes we need to take a little time to arrange it, but by and large, anybody that's wanted to talk to me about anything has talked to me about whatever they want." [8]

On his irritation with the estimated $39 million cost to reissue Idaho's drivers licenses to comply with federal law, and noting that passports are allowed as an alternative form of ID: "I got to thinking, 39 million bucks - I could almost buy everybody in Idaho a passport rather than go through that 39 million bucks . . . [Idahoans are] graciously forgiving. They'll forgive you for making a mistake, but they won't forgive you for not making a decision and move forward. That's what we've tried to do in these seven weeks." [9]

"I am supportive of prekindergarten education, but not at the state level. And let me tell you why. Before you say, 'Well there's ol' Butch again, just like in 1974 when he voted against kindergartens. He hates little kids.' That wasn't it at all. Folks, remember in 1974, we had the same argument in '74 we're having in '07. And that is we are not doing an adequate job now of funding grades half-a-day-of- kindergarten through 12. So when we arrive at a point when we are adequately funding K-12, then we'll consider adding additional burden to that system." [10]

"This is awful important to me. The reforms were well-thought out, vigorously debated and hard-won. And we're right on the precipice of true reform of our educational system. The old educational system was not doing the job. We weren't able to deploy our money and our resources the way we needed to." On pushing for educational reforms including placing limits on collective bargaining rights of teachers. [11]

"And I said, 'Listen, I was born in a family of nine kids in Caldwell, Idaho and I have lived on farms and ranches and raised horses all my life, and I would tell you without any equivocation whatsoever, that if California were my horse, I would shoot it . . . I would put it down. Obviously, easier said than done." To the annual meeting of the Idaho Credit Union League Government Affairs Conference in downtown Boise. [12]

"Obviously because I think it's a violation, not only of our state's rights, but it's a violation of their own oath that they took, when - including Article 1, Section 8 of the Constitution, that pretty well enumerates the powers and the responsibilities of Congress. And there is nowhere that we can find grounded within Article 1, Section 8 an authority to actually write a health care bill that the state of Idaho and the citizens of Idaho are required to take care of." Explaining why Idaho will sue to stop implementation of the Affordable Health Care Act. [13]

"I am right-to-life, I have been a right-to-life candidate in government all my life." Speaking to reporters after signing a law banning abortions after the 20th week of pregnancy. [15]

"Nuclear must be an important part of our energy future. We need to deal with these difficult and challenging issues in a way that the public can embrace." Speaking at a conference of the International Atomic Energy Agency in Salt Lake City [16]

"What the Idaho Health Freedom Act says is that the citizens of our state won't be subject to another federal mandate or turn over another part of their life to government control." [17]

SEAN PARNELL, GOVERNOR OF ALASKA

Governor Sean Parnell was born in Hanford, California in 1962 and moved to Alaska at the age of ten. Parnell was elected Lieutenant Governor of Alaska in 2005 and became governor of Alaska in 2009 after Sarah Palin resigned the governorship. Governor Parnell has served in both the Alaska House of Representatives and Senate. Parnell graduated from Pacific Lutheran University with a degree in Business Administration and went on to earn his J.D. from the University of Puget Sound School of Law. He has owned an Alaska law firm, worked for ConocoPhillips Alaska and for the lobbying firm Patton Boggs. He was elected for a full term governor with 59% of the vote in 2010. He and his wife Sandy have two children.

———————

"[T]he Interior Department's proposal to designate nearly half of Alaska's oil-producing area as critical habitat for the polar bear is a chilling prospect. But it's not chilling in a way that would help the polar bear . . . The only chilling effect would be to Alaska's economy and to the nation's efforts to be energy-independent, an issue critical to our national security." [1]

"I love to have a bowl of [ice cream] at night. And if you put half a gallon of ice cream in the freezer, you can go get the half gallon and you can eat it all in one night, because you like it. Or you can save something for tomorrow. That's what I've done." On why declining oil production means that spending must be limited, despite a huge budget surplus now. [2]

"We need a serious directional change to recover, and merely raising the debt limit will lead only to disaster." [3]

"Only God knows . . . I really don't know. For either one of us to do it is quite speculative." Responding to a question about whether the earth was closer to 6,000 or 6 billion years old. [4]

"Along with more than 41 U.S. senators, the majority of the members of the House, and other governors, I have expressed concern about the recent unrelenting federal attack on states' rights . . . Enough is enough. Alaska has laws to protect its waters. The EPA and Corps of Engineers have no authority to expand their jurisdictions and the state of Alaska will continue to appropriately assert its rights in this arena." [5]

"If you are a state employee who collects a state paycheck and spends it, you are in the oil business." [6]

"We have seen what the status quo looks like and it looks like an empty pipeline . . . Some say we can't afford [my proposed oil tax cuts]. I say we cannot afford doing nothing." [6]

"Thank you for gathering here today for the 12th annual Interdenominational Prayer Service for the unborn. The inalienable right to life is bestowed upon each of us by our Creator, and we cherish the timeless truth that every child is a gift of life, from the moment of conception. On the anniversary of Roe v. Wade, we stand together and recognize the value of human life and pray for those wounded by abortion."

By valuing every life, including the unborn, we strengthen the very fabric of our families and communities, and protect the lives of Alaska's future - our children. May God bless each of you, and may He continue to bless our great state, her people, and our future." [7]

"We believe that any child engaged in prostitution [under the age of 18] is being trafficked, and thus is a victim of a severe and serious crime rather than a prostitute." Upon signing a bill intended to combat human and sex trafficking [8]

"'The world's oldest profession' is, "kind of a nice way of talking about 14- and 13-year olds who are coerced and are dependent on their traffickers for money and for drugs they become hooked upon . . . The director of the Covenant House has called sex and human trafficking, 'calculated torture.' I call it modern day slavery." [9]

"[Oil and gas] tax reductions lead to new production." [9]

"[The Alaska Senate has] just spent half a billion dollars more on education and they have not required results or anything transformational with the system . . . [This funding increase is the] ultimate giveaway." [10]

"I understand some believe free markets, rather than government policy, should direct our investment choices, but this very real threat requires action . . . No free markets exist when one nation builds a nuclear arsenal while it continually and steadfastly advocates for the eradication of an entire nation, with our own not so far behind . . . [A sanction against Iran] comes as a last resort, an option our state has historically refused when presented. However, the time to stand on the principles of life and liberty is at hand, and we must step up along with our country and other states." [11]

"Without language preservation, a culture dies. As Alaskans, we honor and celebrate our traditional cultures. The state will join with Alaskans to make sure these languages live on." Signing a bill to create an Alaska Native Language Preservation and Advisory Council. [12]

"We want to explore more. We have a lot more oil to find. We do not need to depend upon the Middle East as the source of choice. We need to develop our own domestic energy through production here. But we have been stymied by the federal government . . . Republicans and Democrats here support oil exploration and development. They share the belief that we can develop responsibly and create these jobs. I have more difficulty and challenges with the federal administration using the regulatory agencies as an extension of a world view that is different than Alaska's." Speaking to a Conservative Political Action Conference (CPAC) cruise (sponsored in part by theteaparty.net) aboard the Holland America Westerdam in Juneau, Alaska. [13]

"What impact would substantial federal cuts have on us? I say, far less of a hit now then the disaster awaiting us if the federal government continues its current course." [14]

"[W]e have villages in this state where you can pick up the phone, if you're being abused or you're being assaulted, and you won't get help for three or four days, because there is no law enforcement officer in a community with 100 or 200 people, or three hundred people, nor close . . . There are hundreds of communities that are not on any road system. You get there by airplane or by riverboat. That's how you get there. So my goal is that every community in Alaska that wants a law enforcement officer will get one, because statistically and objectively measured, we will reduce the number of assaults in the state. So we've been increasing our numbers of village public safety officers and state troopers to address that." [19]

"If we give every high school student the opportunity for a merit scholarship, if we challenge them to reach higher to take personal responsibility for their futures, many will. These students will transform our economy and positively change the trajectory of Alaska's future for generations. With the Governor's Performance Scholarship proposal, all Alaskan high school students can earn tuition for an in-state university or job-training program. They must complete a more rigorous curriculum than what's now required to graduate from high school. Four years each of math, science, and English and three years of social studies. But for students who take this curriculum, better grades will mean greater tuition awards.

To responsibly pay for these scholarships, I propose saving $400 million, setting it aside and using the interest and investment earnings from this savings account to pay for these yearly scholarships. That way, 30 years from now, we will still have the $400 million but we will also have a workforce better prepared for the future." [15]

"And now, the federal government hyperextends its reach by proposing to zone the oceans. They call it 'marine spatial planning.' But the wild and shifting seas were never meant to be defined by little square boxes of regulated activity. Fish do not check their maps and get their passports stamped as they swim from zone to zone." [15]

"Alaska HAS rare earth minerals. And we ARE strategically located. And now, as you see, we have a GREAT strategic team in place . . . Friends, Alaska is investing in Alaska. With good reason. The global investment climate is shaky. As I look at the world, I don't see a good investment climate. But metals - gold, silver, copper and such, are a solid investment in these times. We are at the brink of a new promise, a promise of rare earth minerals." [16]

"One of the ways we can ensure a more healthy Alaska, and more healthy communities, is to ensure that Alaska Native languages are preserved, restored and revitalized . . . We know that without language preservation, a culture dies. That is intolerable; that is not acceptable. As Alaskans we honor and celebrate our traditional cultures. Today we do this by assuring that the state is now "all in" in making sure that these languages live on." [20]

"Recent events in North Africa and the Middle East have made clear the strategic importance of oil to America's national and economic security. Gasoline prices at the pump are surging, the cost of goods sold will increasingly pull more money from every American's pocket, and our economic recovery, such as it is, is at risk.

This is the moment our federal government must re-examine its "no new wells" policy when it comes to oil exploration and development here at home. The U.S. foolishly imports more than 63 percent of its crude oil, leaving us vulnerable to economic shock from disruption of oil supplies from the international front." [17]

"The irrational set-aside for polar bears has been challenged by the State of Alaska and Alaska Native groups. If allowed to stand, it could have a severe chilling effect on our country's ability to produce more American energy, making us more reliant on foreign oil." [17]

"Because of the work we've done together, Alaskans can now renew their drivers' licenses and ID cards by mail. For our families living off the road system, this DMV improvement is a big convenience. That's something you don't hear often: "DMV" and "convenience" in the same sentence. Only in Alaska!" [18]

"I want to address the challenges to our liberty. When nearly 50,000 Alaskans cast their ballots for statehood in 1958, Governor Hickel said they, 'literally signed a contract. They didn't just say 'yes' to statehood. They agreed to the terms of statehood. And, that contract, like all contracts, cannot be changed without the consent of both parties.' The federal government's expectation, its terms, were that together we Alaskans would develop our resources, build our own economic system, and become largely self-sustaining. We did just that, by logging our timber, mining our minerals and metals, exploring for oil and gas, and harvesting seafood from our waters. These are the engines of our economy: past, present, and future. But today, the federal government owns 240 million acres, almost two-thirds, of Alaska's 371 million acres, and Uncle Sam has posted a virtual 'Keep Out" sign on those lands." [18]

"That U.S. Supreme Court ruling brings to the fore two overarching concerns of Americans - Freedom and keeping their own hard-earned money in their pockets. With growing government health care, Alaskans stand to lose more freedom, and pay more of their hard-earned wages to the federal government in the form of taxes . . . As governor I'm focused on what this means for Alaskans and Alaska." [23]

"A loss borne individually is too great, but, by God's grace, a burden shared can be endured. So, to those of you who have lost a family member, a friend, or a colleague to the sea, including a close friend and colleague of mine, we want you to know that we care for you and stand with you to honor the memory of your loved one.

We're also here to say and pray a blessing upon the fleet. It's about seeking more mercy and safety while upon these waters. And, it's about our hearts of thanksgiving and prayers for more abundance from them. Thank you for sharing this blessing of the fleet and fishermen's memorial as a coastal community, writing the story of our lives together with these waters. Thank you, and God bless." [21]

It's time to stop putting extreme special interests above our people's interests. Where the federal government would lock us out, we will open the doors of opportunity for Alaskans. So long as I am governor, we will not revert to colonial status - and we will not cede control of Alaska's future. [22]

RICK PERRY, GOVERNOR OF TEXAS

Governor James "Rick" Perry was born and raised in Paint Creek, Texas in 1950. Perry graduated from Texas A&M University with a degree in animal science in 1972. He served in the Air Force until 1977, leaving with the rank of Captain. He returned to work in his family's cotton farming business until being elected to Texas House of Representatives in 1984 as a Democrat. In 1990, as a Republican, Perry was elected as the Texas Commissioner of Agriculture in 1990 and again in 1994 before becoming Lieutenant Governor of Texas in 1998. He became Governor of Texas in 2000 when George W. Bush resigned the office to become President of the United States. Perry was elected governor in 2002, 2006, and most recently was re-elected in 2010 with 55% of the vote, and has now become the longest serving Governor of Texas in history. He is the author of the book *Fed Up!: Our Fight to Save America from Washington* and co-authored *On My Honor: Why the American Values of the Boy Scouts Are Worth Fighting For* with Ross Perot. A candidate for the 2012 Republican presidential nomination, Perry suspended his campaign in late January 2012 and endorsed, first, Newt Gingrich, and then Mitt Romney. Governor Perry and his wife Anita have two children.

"With all due respect to anybody that's out there either directly or indirectly criticizing me because I speak plainly, I call it like I see it. Look, I am not an establishment figure, never have been and frankly I don't want to be. I dislike Washington. I think it's a seedy place." Said a few weeks after becoming a presidential candidate. [1]

"Texas is a unique place. When we came into the union in 1845, one of the issues was that we would be able to leave if we decided to do that." "My hope is that America and Washington in particular pays attention. We've got a great union. There's absolutely no reason to dissolve it. But if Washington continues to thumb their nose at the American people, who knows what may come of that." [2]

"It seems right and fitting that the people of Texas should join together in prayer to humbly seek an end to this devastating drought and these dangerous wildfires.   NOW, THEREFORE, I, RICK PERRY, Governor of Texas, under the authority vested in me by the Constitution and Statutes of the State of Texas, do hereby proclaim the three-day period from Friday, April 22, 2011, to Sunday, April 24, 2011, as Days of Prayer for Rain in the State of Texas. I urge Texans of all faiths and traditions to offer prayers on that day for the healing of our land, the rebuilding of our communities and the restoration of our normal and robust way of life." [3]

"I think in America from time to time we have to go through some difficult times, and I think we're going through those difficult economic times for a purpose: to bring us back to those Biblical principles of you know, you don't spend all the money. You work hard for those six years and you put up that seventh year in the warehouse to take you through the hard times. And not spending all of our money. Not asking for Pharaoh to give everything to everybody and to take care of folks because at the end of the day, it's slavery, and we become slaves to government." [4]

"[It']s time for a bold, Texas-style solution to this challenge, that I'm sure the brightest minds in our universities can devise. Today, I'm challenging our institutions of higher education to develop bachelor's degrees that cost no more than $10,000, including textbooks." [5]

"Juarez is reported to be the most dangerous city in America." (Perry later corrected himself.) [6]

"We don't know what the event that has allowed for this massive oil to be released . . . From time to time there are going to be things that occur that are acts of God that cannot be prevented." [7]

"I believe that returning to the letter and spirit of the U.S. Constitution and its essential 10th Amendment will free our state from undue regulations, and ultimately strengthen our Union." "I believe that our federal government has become oppressive in its size, its intrusion into the lives of our citizens, and its interference with the affairs of our state." [8]

"They're sending Washington a message. "We're an independent lot and we just assume Washington not be mortgaging our future." On Tea Party protesters in Texas [8]

"We are fed up with being overtaxed and overregulated. We are tired of being told how much salt we can put on our food, what windows we can buy for our house, what kinds of cars we can drive, what kinds of guns we can own, what kinds of prayers we are allowed to say and where we can say them, what political speech we are allowed to use to elect candidates, what kind of energy we can use, what kind of food we can grow, what doctor we can see, and countless other restrictions on our right to live as we see fit." [9]

"I make a very proud statement and of fact that we have a president that's a socialist. I don't think our founding fathers wanted America to be a socialist country. So I disagree with that premise that, somehow or another, that President Obama reflects our founding fathers. He doesn't. He talks about having a more powerful, more centralized, more consuming and costly federal government." [10]

"I am a tenth amendment believing governor. I truly believe that we need a president that respects the tenth amendment, that pushes back to the states. Whether it's how to deliver education, how to deliver health care, how to do our environmental regulations. The states will considerably do a better job than a one-size-fits-all Washington, D.C., led by this president." [10]

Texans, on the other hand, elect folks like me. You know the type, the kind of guy who goes jogging in the morning, packing a Ruger .380 with laser sights and loaded with hollow-point bullets, and shoots a coyote that is threatening his daughter's dog." [11]

The Obama administration is "leaving American astronauts with no alternative but to hitchhike into space." Perry speaking on the end of the space shuttle era. [12]

"On August the 6th of this year, 2011, we are going to have a day of prayer and fasting. And it's going to be the real deal. It's not going to be some program where we line up a dozen political figures to come in and talk. It's going to be people standing on that stage, projecting and proclaiming Jesus Christ as our Lord and Savior at Reliant Stadium in Houston, Texas. Let me tell you, that's a big stadium and there will be a lot of people. But it's going to send a powerful message across this country!" [13]

"Our country's broke. Well, actually, Washington's broke; our country's going to be just fine. But we've got to have men and women who are willing to stand up to proclaim the values that this country was based upon. In 1774, at the Continental Congress when they got together and penned that first document, they talked about 'life' and 'liberty.' Interestingly, the third thing they talked about was 'property.' A couple of years later, when they actually wrote the Declaration, they changed that 'property' to "'the pursuit of happiness."'" [13]

"I just signed a piece of legislation today, the eminent domain legislation. I tell people, that 'personal property' and the ownership of that personal property is crucial to our way of life. Our founding fathers understood that it was a very important part of the pursuit of happiness. Being able to own things that are your own is one of the things that makes America unique. But I happen to think that it's in jeopardy. It's in jeopardy because of taxes; it's in jeopardy because of regulation; it's in jeopardy because of a legal system that's run amuck. And I think it's time for us to just hand it over to God and say, 'God, You're going to have to fix this.' (*parenthetically*: I think it was Herman Cain who stood up the other day and said, 'How's that 'Hope and Change' thing working out for you?') I think it's time for us to use our wisdom and our influence and really put it in God's hands. That's what I'm going to do, and I hope you'll join me. I hope you'll join us in Houston on the 6th day of August and really start a revival across this country." [13]

"I know from time to time, people will say something like, 'There goes Perry. He wants to secede.' But I love this country. We're a special place. We were created by God-fearing individuals who understood those biblical values and how powerful they could be and would be in the future. And I suggest that for our country, our best days are ahead if we'll get on our knees and ask God to take over and give us wisdom. I may wear the Lord out every day in prayer. I pray for this country. I pray for restoration for this country. I pray for our president every day. I pray that God turns buckets of wisdom out on his head, that God will open his eyes. We can change this country, but it requires our giving it to Him and letting Him guide us." [13]

"[This] loving and personal God desires not a show of religion but a deep connection with our innermost being . . . His agenda is not a political agenda. His agenda is a salvation agenda." [14]

"Father, our heart breaks for America, We see discord at home, we see fear in the marketplace, we see anger in the halls of government. And as a nation, we have forgotten who made us, who protects us, who blesses us.

And for that we cry out for your forgiveness." [14]

"He is a wise, wise God, and he's wise enough to not be affiliated with any political party . . . Father, we pray for our President, that you would impart your wisdom upon him, that you would guard his family. You call us to repent, Lord, and this day is our response."[15]

"Right now, America is in crisis: we have been besieged by financial debt, terrorism and a multitude of natural disasters. As a nation, we must come together and call upon Jesus to guide us through unprecedented struggles and thank him for the blessings of freedom we so richly enjoy." [16]

"Young Hispanics in Texas can aspire to be the next Rolando Pablos, the chairman of the Texas racing commission; maybe the next Roberto de Hoyos, who heads our economic development shop; and one of my favorites, the head of the Texas Alcoholic Beverage Commission Jose Cuevas. Is that awesome? That is the right job for that man." Speaking to the National Association of Latino Elected and Appointed Officials conference in San Antonio [17]

"If this guy prints more money between now and the election, I don't know what y'all would do to him in Iowa, but we . . . would treat him pretty ugly down in Texas. Printing more money to play politics at this particular time in American history is almost treacherous, or treasonous in my opinion." [18]

"What we talked about in the book ['Fed Up!] was that [Social Security] was one of many places where the bureaucrats in Washington D.C. or Congress or president of the United States went well outside our Founding Fathers . . . But look, Social Security is in place, that program is going to be there, it's just got to be transformed, and that's what we're talking about doing." [19]

"I've heard Al Gore talk about man-made global warming so much that I'm starting to think that his mouth is the leading source of all that supposedly deadly carbon dioxide." [20]

"A substantial number of scientists [have] manipulated data to keep the money rolling in . . . I do believe the issue of global warming has been politicized . . . [Scientists are] coming forward daily to disavow a theory that remains unproven." [21]

"Instead of relieving the economic burden . . . you have your counterpart in the United States Senate who is working on a bill that would make things worse for home builders. Under her scheme, federal bureaucrats could take over the local building code enforcement in your city if so-called green mandates are not complied with quickly enough. It is just simply bureaucratic overkill." Speech in New Hampshire, claim rated False by PolitiFact. [22]

"It's a good issue to keep alive. It's fun to poke at him." On raising the issue of whether Barack Obama was born an American citizen. [24]

"Even if an alcoholic is powerless over alcohol once it enters his body, he still makes a choice to drink. And, even if someone is attracted to a person of the same sex, he or she still makes a choice to engage in sexual activity with someone of the same gender." [25]

"It was . . . when the lady who was in [the film, *The Gift of Life*] was looking me in the eye and said 'you really need to think this through.' She said 'I am the product of a rape' and she said 'my life is worth [it].' It was a powerful moment." Discussing how seeing the movie *The Gift of Life* led him to sharpen his position on abortion to oppose it in all circumstances. [26]

"I'm all too aware of government's limitations when it comes to fixing things that are spiritual in nature. That's where prayer comes in. We need it more than ever with the economy in trouble, communities in crisis, people adrift in a sea of moral relativism. We need God's help and that's why I'm calling on Americans to pray and fast like Jesus did." [27]

"Given the trials that have beset our country and world - from the global economic downturn to natural disasters, the lingering danger of terrorism and wars that endanger our troops in Iraq, Afghanistan and theaters of conflict around the globe, and the decline of our culture in the context of the demise of families - it seems imperative that the people of our nation should once again join together for a solemn day of prayer and fasting on behalf of our troubled nation. In times of trouble, even those who have been granted power by the people must turn to God in humility for wisdom, mercy and direction." [28]

"In the spirit of the Book of Joel, Chapter 2, Verses 15-16, I urge a solemn gathering of prayer and fasting. As those verses admonish: 'Blow the trumpet in Zion, declare a holy fast, call a sacred assembly...'Gather the people, consecrate the assembly...As Jesus prayed publicly for the benefit of others in John 11:41-42, so should we express our faith in this way." [28]

"THEREFORE, I invite my fellow Texans to join me on August 6 at Reliant Stadium in Houston, as we pray for unity and righteousness - for this great state, this great nation and all mankind. I urge Americans of faith to pray on that day for the healing of our country, the rebuilding of our communities and the restoration of enduring values as our guiding force. THEREFORE, I, Rick Perry, Governor of Texas, do hereby proclaim August 6, 2011, to be A Day of Prayer and Fasting for Our Nation in Texas, and urge the appropriate recognition whereof." [28]

"Maybe people would want to lock me up. I think about those who talk about Christian faith as being intolerant. Isn't it just the height of intolerance to say you can't gather together in public and pray to our God?" [29]

"People ask me 'What was it like to run for the presidency of the United States?' and I tell them, I say let me tell you, I was the frontrunner for a while and it was the three most exhilarating hours of my life." [30]

"Three and a half years, nearly 100 rounds of golf. Barack Obama has exploded the debt in this country. He has passed a stimulus program that grew government and not the economy. He socialized health care and he armed Mexican drug cartels. Admit it, America, 2008 was our national 'oops' moment." [30]

"I will tell you: It's three agencies of government, when I get there, that are gone: Commerce, Education and the - what's the third one there? Let's see. OK. So Commerce, Education and the - The third agency of government I would - I would do away with the Education, the - Commerce and - let's see - I can't. The third one, I can't. Sorry. Oops." Speaking during a GOP debate, forgetting about his plan to cut the Department of Energy [31]

"Now, you have a President who is using his executive privilege to keep that information from Congress. If that's not Nixonian, then I don't know what it is. We've had over 300 Mexican nationals killed, directly attributable to this Fast and Furious operation, where they brought those guns into Mexico. A former Marine and a Border Patrol agent by the name of Brian Terry lost his life. With Watergate you had a second-rate burglary." [32]

"I would tell you that faith is a major part of who I am. I can't change any more than I can change that I'm the son of two tenant farmers." [33]

"This ruling will be a stomach punch to the American economy. It is a shocking disappointment to freedom-loving Americans desperate to get our country back on track. Obamacare is bad for the economy, bad for health care, bad for freedom. Americans have made clear their overwhelming opposition to its convoluted, burdensome and overreaching mandates.

Freedom was frontally attacked by passage of this monstrosity and the Court utterly failed in its duty to uphold the Constitutional limits placed on Washington. Now that the Supreme Court has abandoned us, we citizens must take action at every level of government and demand real reform, done with respect for our Constitution and our liberty." Statement following the Supreme Court ruling on the Affordable Care Act. [34]

"I have long called for General Holder's resignation over his involvement in the botched Fast and Furious scandal that led to the tragic death of Border Patrol Agent Brian Terry. General Holder's blatant attempts to mislead members of Congress and the American people, paired with his relentless crusade to erode states' rights, have cost him the trust of this nation, and must be stopped." [35]

'You cannot have a conversation about how to deal with the number of illegal individuals who are in this state and our country until you secure the border . . . This president has been in place for three and a half years and I would suggest to you, with signals that he has sent like this last pandering to the Hispanic voters on this immigration issue, that he has made our immigration problem even worse. He sends the signal of come here and you don't have to face any criminal charges or face deportation . . . those that want to talk about immigration reform are wasting our time until they first commit to securing the border." [36]

"How old do I think the earth is. You know what, I don't have any idea. I know it's pretty old - so it goes back a long long ways. I'm not sure anybody actually knows completely and absolutely how long ago the earth is. Your mom is asking about evolution. You know, that's a theory that's out there; it's got some gaps in it. In Texas, we teach both creationism and evolution in our public schools, because I figure you're smart enough to figure out which one is right." Responding to a young boy who asked him who asked him how old Earth is. [37]

"One of the reasons that I'm running for president is I want to make sure that every young man and woman who puts on the uniform of the United States respects highly the president of the United States." [38]

"I'm going to talk to the [people of Iowa] about making Congress a part-time body, just like they have here in Iowa. And I can promise, the people of Iowa think that Washington is spending too much money. They're spending too much time in town. So, make the legislature or I should say the Congress, like their legislature here, part-time and let them come home and have a real job, and work within the citizens, with the citizens and have an opportunity to live within the laws that they pass. And American would be a whole lot better off and I promise you, they will be spending less and getting in less mischief in Washington, D.C." [39]

"Well, obviously, I know there are nine Supreme Court justices. I don't know how eight came out of my mouth. But the fact is, I can't tell you, I don't have memorized all of the Supreme Court judges. Here's what I do know, that when I put an individual on the Supreme Court just like I have done in Texas, we got nine Supreme Court justices in Texas: they will be strict constructionists. They won't be activist judges.

That's what Americans care about. They are not looking for a robot that can spit out the name of every Supreme Court justice, or someone that is going to be perfect in every way. They are looking for somebody who's got values that are based with a deep rudder in the water." [39]

"And I am consistent in my conservative values. I have been consistent. And Americans are looking for someone who is going to make the right decisions, not someone who can either read a teleprompter perfectly or spit out by memory a list of names. That's not what's important to Americans." [39]

"The states ought to be the laboratory of innovation. That is the way our founding fathers had it set up. The Tenth Amendment clearly says that the states are where the action's supposed to be, if you will. And frankly whether Bobby Jindal over there in Louisiana comes up with a great way to deliver health care, trust me I'll go snitch that and move it back to Texas and try it out." [40]

"And that's what the book is really about, it's about freedom. It's about freedom from Washington, D.C., setting the standard, if you will, setting us on a one-size-fits-all course and mentality. And the book is about freedom, freedom from an oppressive Washington tax and regulatory, and a Supreme Court that frankly has been abusing the Constitution as well for way too long." [40] About his book, *Up!: Our Fight to Save America from Washington*

"If anyone was in doubt, we in Texas have no intention to implement so-called state exchanges or to expand Medicaid under Obamacare. I will not be party to socializing healthcare and bankrupting my state in direct contradiction to our Constitution and our founding principles of limited government. I stand proudly with the growing chorus of governors who reject the Obamacare power grab. Neither a 'state' exchange nor the expansion of Medicaid under this program would result in better 'patient protection' or in more 'affordable care.' They would only make Texas a mere appendage of the federal government when it comes to health care." [41]

"George W. Bush did a incredible job in the presidency, defending us from freedom." [42].

"You can always follow me on Tweeter." [43]

"Adios, mofo." Signoff to a satellite interview with San Antonio TV station [44]

RICK SCOTT, GOVERNOR OF FLORIDA

Governor Rick Scott was born in Bloomington, Illinois in 1952 and was raised in Kansas City, Missouri. Scott served in the U.S. Navy and graduated from the University of Missouri-Kansas City with a degree in business administration. He also earned a J.D. from Southern Methodist University. Scott founded the Columbia Hospital Corporation in 1987, merging with the Hospital Corporation of American to form Columbia/HCA in 1989 to become the largest private for-profit health care company in the United States. After Columbia/HCA was charged by the federal Department of Justice with Medicare and Medicaid fraud, Scott resigned from the company, which later was to pay $2 billion in penalties and fines. Scott later founded Richard L. Scott Investments. In his first run for public office, Rick Scott was elected governor in 2010 with 49% of the vote. Governor Scott and his wife Ann have three children.

———————————

"I'm confident that most of us agree that school funding is far more important than spending these dollars on alligator marketing, or boat racing or anything else that the Tallahassee insiders think is so important." [1]

"Let's tell the world, 'If you can dream it, it's easy to make it happen in Florida. After all, we have always been the destination for dreamers. The place where someone with a big new idea could give it a try. Railroads into the wilderness, a magic kingdom, a trip to the moon, freedom from a foreign tyrant, better health, life without winter." [2]

"It's fair to taxpayers. They're paying the bill. And they're often drug screened for their jobs. On top of that, it's good for families. It creates another reason why people will think again before using drugs, which as you know is just a significant issue in our state." [3]

"Clear goals and hard goals can achieve amazing things. The giant oak trees that surround us here. They ARE what they ARE. Because acorns had a plan." [2]

"Taxation, regulation and litigation, those three form the axis of unemployment." [4]

"I ran on a very specific campaign-seven steps to 700,000 jobs-and we did all of those things or are doing all of those things . . . My job is to make sure our state gets back to work, make sure this is the state that's most likely to succeed, and is the most efficient. And we're heading in that direction . . . This is not a popularity contest. I told everybody when I got elected exactly what my plan was . . . to build the private sector. I am following and implementing it, and it's working." [5]

"I remain confident that we're going to start the process of eliminating the business tax. It's clearly the way to get our state back to work." [6]

"Reviewing a government budget is much like going through the attic in an old home. And I'm cleaning it out." [7]

"Get government out of the way of innovation and economic growth, because it is business and the free market that create jobs, not government. Make job creation the No. 1 priority like we have done in Florida by lowering taxes, reducing the size and scope of government, cutting down on frivolous lawsuits and luring companies from around the world to do business here." [8]

"There are a lot of programs that the federal government would like to give you that don't fit your state, don't fit your needs and ultimately create obligations that our taxpayers can't afford . . . I don't want to waste either federal money or state money on something that's unconstitutional. I'd rather nobody run [a health care exchange in Florida]. I don't think there's any way the state can do it where it's good for health care policy." [9]

"Governments don't do a good job deciding what consumers want. They require people to buy things they don't need. There will be policies on there that you may not want to buy but that you'll be forced to buy." [10]

Upon being told the *St. Petersburg Times* would now be called the *Tampa Bay Times*: "That's interesting. Does the region call itself the Tampa Bay region? Is that what it calls itself? The region does?" [11]

"I've ridden elephants, I've never tried to shoot one." Speaking to King Juan Carlos of Spain, who has been attacked in the Spanish press for his elephant hunting trip to Botswana. [12]

"[Florida doesn't need] a lot more anthropologists in this state. It's a great degree if people want to get it. But we don't need them here. I want to spend our money getting people science, technology, engineering and math degrees. That's what our kids need to focus all of their time and attention on: Those type of degrees that when they get out of school, they can get a job."[13]

"I got accused of not liking anthropologists the other day. But just think about it, how many more jobs do think there are for anthropologists in the state? Do you want to use your tax dollars to educate more people who can't get jobs in anthropology? I don't. I want to make sure that we spend our dollars where people can get jobs when they get out." [14]

"Journalists. How many more jobs are there in journalism? Is it the easiest place to get a job right now?" [15]

Some of these universities are wanting to raise tuition 15 percent a year. I mean, name a business. Can you raise your advertising rates 15 percent year after year? You can't. You wouldn't be in business. Your competition wouldn't let you." [16]

"President Obama's latest observation that job creation efforts have been hindered because America has been 'lazy' in attracting investment is clearly incorrect. To characterize the efforts of American businesses and Governors throughout the nation who are working hard to build jobs in this way is not only wrong but stands in the way of their efforts to sell the value of our great nation every day. I recently returned from Brazil, where I and dozens of Florida business leaders worked hard to attract jobs to America . . . Obstacles to job creation in America are a result of policy, not of motivation. Our business taxes are among the highest in the world. Our regulations are among the most difficult in the world. If you need evidence, look no further than the companies who have moved their oil rigs from the Gulf coast to foreign countries in the last year because of the regulatory environment." [17]

"We shouldn't be allowing candidates to attack people in business. We should be saying, gosh, that's us." [18]

"We've got to defend the freedom of the free market. If we don't defend the free market, they'll pick on somebody. Now they're picking on Bain Capital, then they'll pick on somebody else . . . When you see somebody being attacked because they live the American dream, we ought to go out and say, 'Gosh, I'd like to live the American dream.'" While paraphrasing the famous Niemoller quote "First they came for the Jews . . . " to defend Mitt Romney against attacks. [18]

"Please, Mr. President, help us bring jobs to America and let us have an honest conversation about the barriers in our way." [17]

"Our state workers don't pay for anything into their pension plan. And we can't afford that; it's not fair to taxpayers. If you didn't have collective bargaining, would it be better for the state? Absolutely . . . [In limiting public employee bargaining rights, Governors Walker and Kasich are] absolutely doing the right thing." [19]

"If you want to fix the system, and you actually want to make sure that people get health care, then use the free market." [20]

"I will continue to work tirelessly on making positive changes to our business climate in Florida until we achieve my goal of making this state the No. 1 business destination in the world." [21]

"I still believe the federal government ought to secure our borders. They ought to have a national immigration policy and take responsibility for this. I think the states have had to respond because the federal government hasn't." [22]

"Unless my wife tells me she's dumping me, I'm running for a second term." [23]

"It shows you, if you go make the tough choices, and you do exactly what you said when you ran, you will get re-elected. That is exactly what Governor Walker did. He went and made the tough choices. We've got to start living within our means. Make sure you treat people with respect, but you cannot be wasting state dollars. That is exactly what we're doing here . . . That is why he won." Speaking after Scott Walker's 2012 recall election victory in Wisconsin. [24]

"If we're a better place to do business, people are going to flock to Florida." [26]

When asked if he believes in global warming: "I have not been convinced. " As to what would persuade him: "Something more convincing than what I've read." [25]

"I am honored today to sign four bills that strengthen Florida's pro-life laws. During my campaign and since I have been governor, I have made it very clear that I am, and always have been, pro-life." [27]

"I don't know the purpose of Occupy Wall Street, but I like the fact that people are active. I don't know what the goals are, but the fact that people are active in the political process, I think it's great."[26]

"I haven't seen the bill, but I believe in Jesus Christ, and I believe individuals should have a right to say a prayer." Reacting to a bill that would allow students to offer "inspirational messages," including prayers, at school events." [28]

"We can't allow frivolous suits and unreasonable awards to give our state a reputation that frightens away new jobs." [29]

"It is unclear how disarming law-abiding citizens would better protect them from the dangers and threats posed by those who would flout the law." May 1, 2012 letter to Tampa Mayor Bob Buckhorn rejecting Buckhorn's request to ban guns downtown during the 2012 Republican National Convention there. [30]

"Think of how exciting it will be when our schools are recruiting our children, when every school in the state focuses on continual improvement in order to outperform every other school in attracting students. I am calling for an increase in the number of charter schools, public schools that are allowed to work independently of school boards and can innovate in ways that encourage all schools to improve." [29]

"I ask everyone to look beyond the short-term and imagine with me what Florida will look like when we turn our state around. Such a moment may not come again." [29]

"I love people. Some people get energized around people and ideas, policies and stuff like that. I love that stuff." [23]

RICK SNYDER, GOVERNOR OF MICHIGAN

Governor Rick Snyder was born in Battle Creek, Michigan in 1958. Snyder earned a Bachelor's, MBA and J.D. from the University of Michigan, all by the time he was 23. He was President and COO of computer giant Gateway and was also CEO, chairman of the board, and a co-founder of Ardesta, LLC, an Ann Arbor based venture capital firm. Never having held elected office before, Snyder ran for governor in 2010. Snyder dubbed himself, "One Tough Nerd" and was elected with 58% of the vote. He and his wife Sue have three children. Governor Snyder's law on emergency financial managers, who can take over city matters from elected officials, faces a referendum in November 2012.

"We need to move from negative to positive. We need to stop looking in the rearview mirror and look toward the future. We need to stop being divisive and become inclusive." [1]

"It is about us all working together. Lansing and state government will not be the solution to all our problems. Ten million people working together is the key." [1]

"I've been hired to represent all of the people of the State of Michigan, and to move us all forward together. It will require shared sacrifice from all of us." [1]

"Three cookies for breakfast every day." Discussing how he started his mornings at college (eating cookies sent by his mother), while eating a cookie sample at a farmer's market at the Capitol in Lansing [2]

"[Martin Luther King] talked about poverty, racism, and militarism. With respect to poverty, we do need to solve poverty, and we need to get barriers out of the way . . . We have four of the highest crime cities in the country in our state, and that's unacceptable . . . We need to step up, because that is part of the cycle of poverty and racism. And one of the best answers for solving the crime problem isn't simply law enforcement, that's an important one, but it's helping people have a job. If you have a job, you don't end up on the crime side . . . The most important thing we can do is help people get a job. And it shouldn't just be a job that goes nowhere. It should be a job that's a career. We're working hard on that." [3]

"I was a victim of bullying. I was bullied in elementary school, in middle school and in high school because I was a nerd . . . Bullying is just wrong and bad."[4]

"Today is marking the death of the Michigan Business Tax. It's about more and better jobs, and creating an environment for our young people to stay in Michigan." [5]

"WHEREAS, though Pi is never ending, it is often limited to 3.14, and that is why we celebrate Pi and Pie Day on March 14; and,

WHEREAS, on this day, we raise awareness and reiterate the vital role math and science education plays in the lives of our children, but we also encourage Michigan citizens to eat a piece of pie or pot pie made with fresh fruits or vegetables grown right here in our great state;

NOW, THEREFORE, I, Rick Snyder, Governor of Michigan, do hereby proclaim March 14, 2011 as Pi and Pie Day in Michigan." [6]

"Traditional politicians like to talk about policy a lot. Actually traditional politicians talk too much in my view. They get into policy issues and how to keep on making policy after policy after policy. I don't view that as the best answer. It's really figuring out what makes a difference and be consistent." [7]

"I think a lot of the Midwest should all want to come back together, so that it's not one state versus another state. In many respects, the Midwest was treated as flyover territory and we're a great place to be, for quality of life and everything else." [7]

"Here you have people who are coming to get a Ph.D. in engineering at the University of Michigan or Michigan State, and then we tell them to leave. That's dumb, to be blunt. This isn't talking about solving every issue related to immigration, but there's no reason for anyone to be against [supporting a special immigration program for immigrants with science-technology-engineering backgrounds] once the facts are laid out in front of them. This is an exercise in relentless positive action, of trying to get Washington to adopt this methodology to say, 'There is no blame. There is no credit. There's common ground. We all agree. Let's just put in a solution and go.'" [7]

"This legislation furthers the goal of good government by promoting greater transparency and ensuring that public resources are used solely for their intended purposes. It is essential that state public school resources be devoted to the education of our children. This continues the fiscal reforms designed to save schools money and help them operate even more efficiently." [8]

"I never want to be anyone's enemy, but if the end result is the City of Detroit has a consent agreement, financial stability and better services, so be it . . . I would not have any expectation of short-term cash assistance from the state . . . We need long-term solutions, we need structural solutions . . . Detroit is not alone in having . . . high legacy costs [related to issues such as pension and retiree health care obligations]." [9]

"I'm going to hold the olive branch out. I would hope that after an initial reaction [to the proposal] that people step back and say: 'Is this the best path to get us to be successful?' This is not about fighting or about having someone lose, but about how we can all say this is a better answer for all of us." On discussions with Detroit leaders on a proposed consent agreement to deal with Detroit's fiscal problems. [10]

"If you know someone that's got a challenge, is the right answer they tell you to go away? Or should they hold up their hand and say, 'Please come help?' The inclination so far has been to say, 'Go away.' I don't believe that's a good answer." [11]

"The citizens of Detroit want solutions. They want to be able to get on a bus on time. They want the police to show up. They want some basics. We want to be a supportive resource in the state to partner with the city - not run the city - to achieve success . . . This is really focusing on letting the city run the city while having stronger financial management and stability for the long-term. This isn't about the current people in office. This is about long-term stability and to make sure we implement things."[12]

"If you change the rules for one [city], everyone could do a casino. Everyone will do a casino. Then nobody wins." [13]

"It's not an us versus them. We're all in this together. Doesn't everyone want to see Detroit succeed?" [14]

"There is too much crime, and these shootings in Detroit are very troubling . . . The best solution to crime is not to have it happen, and if you can help people have a job, that breaks that cycle." [15]

"These dilapidated properties are often occupied by drug or other criminal operations or simply held by speculators willing to perpetuate community blight in the hope of personal financial gain . . . [Our plan] will encourage current property owners to clean up and prevent blight on their property, and also prevent bad actors from degrading good neighborhoods." Discussing his plan to bar people with unpaid tax bills from buying land at county foreclosure auctions. [16]

"We've Americanized these companies and forgotten they were created by immigrants who have given our communities so much. We need to embrace different people and different cultures. All of us are from different places if you go back far enough. That's what we need to remind people of." [17]

Regarding the immigration system that allows foreign students with talent to study here and forces them to leave when they are done. "How dumb is that? Let's ask them to stay . . . We've lost our way and we need to go back to fundamentals and say we're the place that welcomes everyone. That's how you lead the world." [17]

"We want to create an environment where Michiganders can feel good about coming downtown for dinner. You want them to go to the ball game and have fun." Unveiling an anticrime plan in Flint, Michigan, March 7, 2012. [18]

"Our state will continue to struggle until we tackle the problems of our most violent cities. The entire state pays the price when tourists are hesitant to visit our cities, when businesses and talented people are reluctant to consider locating in Michigan and when everyone's insurance rates rise . . . We need a comprehensive approach to public safety that offers increased economic activity for our children and their parents in our distressed communities to break the cycle of crime." [19]

"In terms of how do we change the culture in some of these communities that have the highest crimes is a real challenge, but it's something that you go after. Because, I'm trying to change the whole culture of the state . . . A lot of it is showing them a path to a positive future. A comprehensive approach lets them feel safer with what they do by having more law enforcement. Let's do things in criminal justice that both deal with specific categories of mental health and drug issues, along with better victim protections with seniors and situations with human trafficking. And then, let's look at crime prevention where we can focus on structurally unemployed to help them get a real job. Not a short-time, make-work job, a real job and then get them on a career path." [20]

"That's unacceptable. We need to put a focus on that . . . so I believe it's appropriate to make a significant investment in public safety." Referring to Detroit, Flint, Pontiac and Saginaw all placing in the top 10 in crime for American cities over 50,000 people. [21]

"[Michigan is now] the poster child for good policy." [22]

"We're coming back strong because we're going to have the leadership we need in Washington. I just got back from there and it's a mess." Speaking at Mitt Romney's victory party after the 2012 Michigan presidential primary. [23]

"I'm not going to go armchair quarterback it. I think there are alternative scenarios that could have worked also, but the point is, is that it's history, and the important part is it was successful, we're moving along, creating jobs." On ABC's "This Week" in February 2012, discussing his support for the automaker bailout, a policy at odds with Mitt Romney's position. [24]

"While graduate student research assistants provide valuable efforts for universities, they are students first and foremost. Considering them to be public employees with union representation would alter the nature of the critical relationship between students and teachers, and risk the educational mission of universities." Press release on signing bill declaring graduate student employees are not considered public employees and are therefore ineligible to unionize. [25]

"My concern is that could start a whole divisive atmosphere of other people trying to put right-to-work on the ballot, a whole bunch of things like that, and that would distract from the good things we've got going on." Urging labor unions and their allies not to pursue a state constitutional amendment that would guarantee a right of collective bargaining. [26]

On political conflicts over labor issues in neighboring Wisconsin, Indiana and Ohio: "I think it's unfortunate that they've gotten to that, I don't want to see that happen. If you want to draw it as a contrast, you look at now that they've had those things happen, do they have a productive environment to solve problems? Not necessarily. They're still overcoming the divisiveness, the hard feelings from all of that . . . I think I'm fairly unique around the country. I call my approach relentless positive action and it's worked well; we're showing great results. " [27]

"The people of Michigan have repeatedly spoken on this issue and this legislation reaffirms the value of human life. It also brings Michigan in line with federal law." Statement on signing a partial-birth abortion ban into law [28]

"I am not a big fan of casinos. I recognize them for their entertainment value, but you have to look at the other community impacts that come with them." [29]

"It doesn't matter. It's not about me, it's about Michigan being a great state again. That's why I wanted this job, that's why I took this job and let's just get the job done and go." On being told by interviewer Charlie Langton that he had a right to brag about his accomplishments as governor. [30]

On dealing with Detroit's problems: "We're there to be a positive resource. And these problems go back for decades, so this isn't a recent thing, so I appreciate the mayor and the city council taking on some of these issues because this is not a new thing, this is a 40 or 50 year issue. But the thing is, we need action . . . I'm not there to run the City of Detroit. I'm there to be a supportive partner and a practical partner that wants to get involved and do things and help and then just say "Let's go, and go, and go." [30]

"Unemployment among veterans in Michigan is about 30 percent, and that's simply unacceptable." [31]

On why he supported a state income tax cut: "Those are taxpayer dollars. Shouldn't we give it back to the people that gave it to us? Shouldn't we give it back to the hard-working people of the State of Michigan?" [32]

"[My first two years as Governor have been about] defining who we are, why we're here and what we're really trying to do. What's government supposed to do? The role of government isn't to be an ATM machine and give out money." [32]

"We're the comeback state, but we've got a lot of work to do." [32]

"The role of government is to serve you. The role of government is to show you you're getting a real return on what you invest. We're just another shopping choice for you and you have to figure out how much government you want to buy." [32]

"The underlying key to success . . . is to change our culture. We need to move from negative to positive. We need to stop looking in the rear view mirror and look toward the future. We need to stop being divisive and become inclusive. We have spent too much time fighting among ourselves and become our own worst enemy. This will not be simple or easy. There are no magic solutions to our problems. But with most problems, there also comes opportunity." [33]

"We are having great success here in Michigan, but we have a problem. We Michiganders are too humble. We don't brag well . . . It's time for us not to brag, not to be arrogant, but to point out the fact that we are back. Now is not the time to be satisfied. I certainly am not satisfied with our present state. We need to be accelerating. We have to avoid complacency, we have to avoid being content." [31]

"When we make changes like this, we are faced with the realization many of us will have to take a step back in the short term to move us all forward together in the long term." [33]

"[When Michigan's economy was in worse shape, neighboring states] didn't care about us. Now they're actually saying bad things about us, saying we're all messed up. I view that as good progress." [34]

"We had the natural resources era in the 1800s. We had the industrial era in the 1900s. We led the world in both eras. It's time to do it again. It's time for the era of innovation." [35]

On helping local governments who would lose revenue with his proposed repeal of taxes on business equipment: "The goal is not to harm them. The goal is to partner with them, so we can all succeed, watch more jobs come, watch the companies succeed, watch the communities grow." [35]

"Career politicians are often more concerned with immediate political ramifications than they are with finding long-term solutions. My goal as governor is to fundamentally reinvent Michigan by making lasting reforms so we are in better shape 10, 20, 30 years from now. To be blunt, I couldn't care less what the polls say in the meanwhile." [38]

"Too many students are being forced to move back home with their parents after graduating because they can't find a job . . . Mitt Romney's plan to align higher education with the needs of the job market is on the right track. Simplifying the student loan process and giving students the tools they need to make informed decisions will help ensure they are able to start their careers without being saddled with massive debt. Here in Michigan, we approved tenure reform legislation that makes it easier to reward great teachers and remove ineffective ones from the classroom. We also recently approved changes that will give parents and students more choices about where to attend school, including expanding options for online classes. Mitt Romney will bring ideas like these to the national stage. As a proud nerd, I'm encouraged by Mitt Romney's education reform plan." [36]

"Last year no one thought we could get the budget balanced by June. This year, no one is surprised that we did it again. Pay attention, Washington, D.C." [37]

"According to the non-partisan U.S. Bureau of Labor Statistics, there are 111,647 more people working in Michigan today than when I took office. That's enough to fill U of M's Big House [Michigan Stadium]." [39]

"The Affordable Care Act is not the law I would have enacted, but it is the law that we have. Yes, it is possible that it will be repealed and that Washington will change course, but we cannot bury our heads in the sand until that day comes. We have the opportunity to act now and create a health exchange that works for the people of Michigan, and that's an opportunity we should take." [40]

"Will be on MSNBC's "Morning Joe" Friday at 7 am to talk about how fiscally conservative policies are taking our state from the bottom to the top. The nation is starting to notice the positive changes that are happening here." [41]

"Michigan is doing well, but Detroit is not participating the way I would like, and we need to do something about it . . . We need a vision. This cannot simply be about making things less worse. We need something that can develop fire, passion and excitement . . . " [42]

"I am probably the most pro-immigration governor in the United States. I think we need to go back to what made us a great country before, which is encouraging people to move and stay in the U.S." [43]

"I asked for a lot of change. People tend to like change until it actually arrives." [22]

"The rest of the country is too used to looking at Detroit as a place where people are fighting one another." [42]

"[We should be] positive, forward thinking and inclusive. Did you ever see blame solve a problem?" [44]

SCOTT WALKER, GOVERNOR OF WISCONSIN

Governor Scott Walker was born in Colorado Springs, Colorado in 1967 and grew up in Plainfield, Iowa and Delavan, Wisconsin. Walker attended Marquette University, but withdrew during his senior year and never graduated. Governor Walker was the County Executive of Milwaukee County, Wisconsin and before that served for nine years in the Wisconsin State Assembly. He was elected governor in 2010 with 52% of the vote. Governor Walker's efforts on the budget and restrictions on collective bargaining for public employees sparked weeks of demonstrations and a series of recall elections. Over two elections, three Republican state senators were recalled, tipping the balance of the chamber to Democrats. Walker himself won a recall election in 2012 with 53% of the vote. Governor Walker and his wife Tonnette have two children.

———————

"You have given us a mandate for true reform, and I appreciate that. I will not let you down . . . Tonight, I want to tell every worker, every family and every business, big or small in this state, that you have an ally in the governor's office." Victory speech in general election, November 2, 2010. [1]

"Years ago Wisconsin had a tourism advertising campaign targeted to Illinois with the motto, 'Escape to Wisconsin.' Today we renew that call to Illinois businesses, 'Escape to Wisconsin.' You are welcome here." [2]

"And I stood up and I pulled out a picture of Ronald Reagan, and I said, you know, this may seem a little melodramatic, but 30 years ago, Ronald Reagan . . . had one of the most defining moments of his political career, not just his presidency, when he fired the air-traffic controllers. And, uh, I said, to me that moment was more important than just for labor relations or even the federal budget, that was the first crack in the Berlin Wall and the fall of Communism because from that point forward, the Soviets and the Communists knew that Ronald Reagan wasn't a pushover." From the transcript of conversation between Walker and the blogger who pretended to be billionaire conservative David Koch. [3]

"We went in to solve our problems in Wisconsin and we did . . . "Anytime you have a crisis you can either let it overcome you or you can take it head-on . . . If they think I'm caving they've been asleep for the last eight years because I've taken on every major battle in Milwaukee County and won, even in a county where I'm overwhelmingly overpowered, and because I don't budge." More from the conversation with "David Koch."[3]

"I have [a baseball bat] in my office; you'd be happy with that. I got a Slugger with my name on it." Even more from the conversation with "David Koch."[3]

"They defined [collective bargaining] as a rights issue. It's not a rights issue. It's an expensive entitlement . . . With every day, week and month that goes by that the world doesn't fall apart," the furor over the bargaining law subsides. Where has the polarization come from, where have the attacks come from? They haven't come from anything we've said." [4]

"When people ask me, 'How do you appeal to Tea Party folks?' I say: I was the original Tea Party in Wisconsin. Eight years ago we held recalls. We got rid of a county executive who had been in office almost since the time I was born." [4]

"Any time you're going to make a bold move, challenging the status quo, you're going to face passion. If given the choice to stand with [those protesting] or to stand with the good, hard-working taxpayers all across Wisconsin, many of whom are paying much more for health care and benefits than the modest amount we're asking for in this proposal, I'm going to stand with the hard-working taxpayers of Wisconsin." [5]

"I would like to thank Governor Quinn for coming to Kenosha this morning to serve at the Shalom Food Pantry. I look forward to having him back when the Green Bay Packers repeat as Super Bowl champions." To Illinois Governor Pat Quinn, who spent a morning working in a Wisconsin food pantry wearing a Packers jersey to pay off a bet he lost to Walker when the Packers beat the Bears in the 2010 NFC Championship game. [6]

"Here in Wisconsin, we don't need a seating chart to bring Republicans and Democrats together - all we need are the Green Bay Packers. " [7]

"I don't know [if voters will vote to recall me]. I'll leave that up to the pundits. To me, what I'll be judged on - whether it's next year or 2014 - is ultimately going to be how successful we are on our campaign to create 250,000 jobs in the state." [8]

"[Voters] also told us not just in Tuesday's results but I think they told us in the months leading up to it, they want us to do more to work together and so that's exactly what we're going to do." On the 2011 recall elections in which four Republican state senators retained their seats, but two were recalled. [9]

"After these recalls, my guess is it'll be a long time - again, regardless of party - before at least a large number of people pursue recalls, because they've just had it. They've had it with the ads." After the 2011 recall elections [10]

"Here's a problem. Here's a solution. Now go out and do it. I've got a clear agenda and I try to get it done." [11]

"Last November, the voters sent a message that they wanted fiscal responsibility and a focus on jobs. In our first months in office we balanced a $3.6 billion deficit and our state created 39,000 new jobs. It's clear the voters also want us to work together to grow jobs and improve our state.

With that in mind, earlier this evening I reached out to the leadership of both the Republicans and Democrats in the Assembly and State Senate. I shared with them that I believe we can work together to grow jobs and improve our state. In the days ahead I look forward to working with legislators of all parties to grow jobs for Wisconsin and move our state forward." Statement after two Republican state senators were removed in recall elections in August 2011 [12]

"The mistake I made early on is, I looked at it almost like the head of a small business: identify a problem, identify a solution and go out and do it . . . I don't think we built enough of a political case, so we let . . . the national organizations come in and define the debate while we were busy just getting the job done." [15]

"We are ready to take on the liberals in Madison . . . Together we can put the government back on the side of the people again . . . You don't have to be afraid anymore because help is on the way . . . Our plan: Lowering taxes and cutting through the red tape." From victory speech in Republican gubernatorial primary, September 2010. [13]

Responses to questions during testimony before U.S. House of Representatives Committee on Oversight and Government Reform, April 14, 2011. [Source 14]:

How much money does requiring an annual vote for union representation save the state of Wisconsin?" "That particular part doesn't save any." [14]

"How much does prohibiting employees from paying union dues from paychecks save the state of Wisconsin?" "It would save employees up to $1000 per year they could use to pay for pensions and health care contribution . . . It's to give workers a right. It's to give workers the right to choose." [14]

"Are you ready to apologize to the people of Wisconsin for hiring the son of a donor, Brian Deschane, to an administration position when better qualified candidates had also applied?" "That person was five levels below me. When that hiring was brought to my attention I had my staff go back and have that person taken out of that position and I acknowledge the fact that there are more qualified people and I asked another person be put into that." [14]

"Will you pay a price due to the approach you took?" "If you're going to participate in democracy you have to be in the arena. When 14 of my colleagues in the Capitol decided to leave for three weeks it made it very difficult to do that." [14]

"When I look at what Mitch Daniels did six years ago in Indiana, he did what we're proposing to do. His numbers were far below mine in the first six months he was in office. He was dealing with some of the same passions, but not as big because he did it through executive order, not through a piece of legislation. Four years later he was reelected with 58 percent of the vote, because in the end people saw the results." [14]

"Did you explicitly single out collective bargaining during your campaign for Governor?" "No." [14]

"You might concede that some might be surprised then that you made collective bargaining such a centerpiece of your reform efforts after you were sworn in?" "I'd say no, because for eight years as county executive I not only talked about it I actually did what I called a "reality tour" where I talked about the challenges and that we were unsustainable and that collective bargaining was driving that." [14]

"Were you surprised by the response in your state?" "Not in my state. For eight years I took on the status quo in a county that's never elected a Republican before. I was elected with 54, then 57, then 59 percent because I think in times of crisis people aren't so much concerned about Republican or Democrat, they want leadership. That's what we're trying to do at the state level. What did surprise me, candidly, was the level of national attention, the people who came in from Washington and others to be part of that debate." [14]

"What did you mean when you said it would be outstanding for the fake David Koch to fly you out to 'Cali'"?" "At that point I was done with the call, I had two other people waiting for me, and I was trying to get off the call and get onto the next issue." [14]

"Are teachers paid too much or too little?" "If we could set up a system where we rewarded based on performance and merit, I'd even be willing to pay more, but we don't have that system currently, we have one solely based on seniority." [14]

"Do you believe your actions were extreme?" "No, because I believe fundamentally if what we've heard said over and over again was a fundamental right you all in Congress would be acting on it now. You do not have collective bargaining, other than postal service workers, for the vast majority of public employees who work for the federal government for wages and for benefits. If it's a fundamental right why aren't you debating it right here and now. It's a government entitlement. Collective bargaining is important for the private sector, for the examples we've heard about the impacts it's had on families and legacies. Private sector unions are my partners in economic development, I work with them and I hope to work with our public employees. But collective bargaining itself is not a fundamental right, rights come from the Constitution and no where in the Constitution is that clearly defined." [14]

"And if we fail to win, it will take us down the path we see, failing, people like the people in Illinois, down in Springfield, and I for one don't want that. Not because this job is that important to me, 'cause frankly my wife in some ways would love it if I'd go back to the private sector and make some real money." [16]

"Every time I tried to do something sensible to balance our budget without laying people off, the unions said no." Referring to battles with labor unions during his time as Milwaukee County Executive. [17]

Reporter David Brody: "Where does God fit into all of this, because as as a 'PK' [Preacher's Kid] as you called yourself earlier, look, there's got to be peace there, at the root of all of this for you?"

Governor Scott Walker: "Oh, absolutely. People ask all the time, to [my wife] Tonette and I, how do you get through this? It's just really prayer. It's the prayers that we have as a family, that we have individually, and the prayers that people tell us about. And those that we don't even hear about, but we feel people all around our state and really all around the country, that people go out of their way to lift us up, and it's just, it has been so amazing to us, and really as a family, I think it has made us stronger. We realize that all this is just a temporary thing and God's got a plan for us that, who knows where it might be, beyond just serving as Governor of this state, but if we stay true to that, there's always comfort." [18]

Brody: "How important is your victory on June 5th as it relates to the Tea Party movement? There are going to be a lot of folks that say look, if you lose they're going to say we took down a tea party guy who tried to do his tea party agenda, And we took him down. What will it say about the tea party if you actually win on June 5th?"

Walker: "I think it goes even beyond, even more fundamental than that. What I think it does is when we prevail it sends a powerful, powerful message not just here in my statehouse, but in Springfield, in Columbus, in Albany and Austin and Tallahassee and state houses all across America, and equally if not more so, it says to Washington DC and people like my friend Paul Ryan and others who are trying to tackle tough issues as well it sends a powerful message that voters are saying, yeah, we do want leaders to stand up and do the right thing. We do want them to tackle the tough issues. Conversely, God help us if we fail, I think it sets aside any kind of courage in American politics for at least a decade, if not a generation and that's why I say all the time, that's why we can't fail." [18]

"I think it's flat out about intimidation . . . [T]he unions . . . want people to live in fear of challenging any of these status quo items again in the future." [18]

––––––––––––––––

"[I am proud of] trying to defund Planned Parenthood and make sure they didn't have any money, not just for abortion, but money for anything." Speaking to Wisconsin Right to Life, April 2010. [19]

[Mandating that women getting an abortion must meet privately with a doctor before the procedure is] "pro-health and pro-women." Speaking at Golden House, a Green Bay shelter for domestic abuse victims. [20]

"The advocates for big government view me as a threat. They want to take me out and they want to take me out before anybody else across America dares to take them on when it comes to big government. [I signed a castle doctrine law because] we want to make sure you can protect not only your home, but that you can protect your loved ones." Speaking to the National Rifle Association convention in St. Louis, April 2012. [22]

"In the past, lawyers could clog up the legal system. Instead, the state Department of Workforce Development gets to be the one that ultimately can put people back and give them up to two years back pay if there is reason to believe there was pay discrimination in the workforce." Defending his repeal of a state equal pay law [23]

When asked if other states would suffer the sort of financial upheaval Greece is facing if they do not take the sorts of measures to curb collective bargaining and budgets Walker pursued: "I think that's what's at stake anywhere across the country if we don't fix these things . . . In contrast, we've made it work in Wisconsin. We've lowered our overall tax burden, we ultimately saw a net increase in jobs this year, we've seen long-term structural reforms that allowed us to balance our budget, and I think we can do that across the country." [24]

"I think you'll see the most radical elements on the left are going to be involved in this recall, because again for them, this is so critically important. I think they understand that when we win, this will send a powerful message not just to other Republican governors, but to even some of the discerning Democrats who hold governorships and even mayoral positions across the country." [25].

Laughing off suggestions that he has become a "GOP rock star": "I've got two high school sons who would beg to differ with anybody calling me anything related to rock star. They see me at Summerfest, the world's largest music festival in Milwaukee, and jokingly say I go to the old fogey stage." [25]

"This one's obviously special." Commenting on how proud he was to sign a voter ID law; he had introduced such legislation as a state House member. [21]

"The left, the radical left, and the big labor union bosses are somehow counting on the idea that they can bring enough money and enough bodies into Wisconsin to dissuade voters . . . I think that they're hoping somehow they can defeat us, so that would discourage anybody from making tough decisions again . . . And like I said, I'm an optimist. I think we'll win, and I think when we do, it will open the door to people being more courageous." [26]

"I firmly believe you're going to see a dramatic takeoff after June 5th, because businesses feel like we're headed in the right direction. I think the big thing that people are waiting for is to have the certainty of knowing that this sort of positive outlook for job creators is going to continue . . . That's why I think that after June 5th, after these primaries are done, and when I and the lieutenant governor and these senators prevail, I think it means there will be a clear message to the job creators and the small businesses in the state that now is the time to add jobs. And I think they will." Arguing that winning his recall election would lead to a surge in jobs. [27]

"As you'll see in the next four and a half weeks, I'm going to run an election to win. I'm working hard to win. I'm making my case around the state. But I'm not afraid to lose. The reason I say that is five years from now, whether my name is on the outside of the governor's office, local governments and people across the state could look back and say, 'We didn't just fix things, we made them better.'" [28]

"You see, when we prevail, God willing and with the help of voters June 5th, this will send a powerful message and not just to Madison. Conversely, if we lose, which is obviously possible in a 50-50 race, I think it sets aside any courage - Republicans or Democrats alike - in politics for at least a decade." [28] Walker also predicted that if he, Lt. Gov. Rebecca Kleefisch and the Republican senators facing recall lost their races, the state would be plunged into what he termed "recall pingpong." "It will go back and forth. I don't think that's just bad for elections, it's bad for jobs." [28]

"It's not going to come to my desk, plain and simple . . . I don't think there is any real interest from the vast majority of lawmakers, be they Republican or Democrat, of going through the next session what we went through earlier this past year." In response to a question about whether he would veto right-to-work legislation if it came to his desk [28]

"I live on a busy street, and half the cars are going by pretty fast. One of them honked. And I looked, the guy had rolled down his window, put his arm out, and flipped me off . . . What I usually do is, I pray for them. There's probably something more troubling in their life, than whether they agree with me or not. And besides, if you stay positive, something will come along . . . And there's not one, but there's two cars, both honking and both rolling their arms out. And just as I think the same thing is going to happen again, they give me a thumbs-up." [29]

"My wife said she used to hear from people that are frustrated at seeing the 'Recall Walker' signs - until someone reminded her that 'recall' is another word for 'remember.' So they remember Walker, and remember to pray for us." [29]

Diane Hendricks: "Any chance we'll ever get to be a completely red state and work on these unions "

Governor Scott Walker: "Oh, yeah"

Hendricks: "- and become a right-to-work? What can we do to help you?"

Walker: "Well, we're going to start in a couple weeks with our budget adjustment bill . . . The first step is we're going to deal with collective bargaining for all public employee unions, because you use divide and conquer. So for us, the base we get for that is the fact that we've got - budgetarily we can't afford not to. If we have collective bargaining agreements in place, there's no way not only the state but local governments can balance things out . . . That opens the door once we do that. That's your bigger problem right there." Conversation with Beloit billionaire Diane Hendricks, one of Walker's leading financial supporters at ABC Supply (Hendricks' company) for a meeting of Rock County 5.0, an economic development group, January 11, 2011. [30]

"Tonight, you might say I'm preaching to the choir with a bunch of fellow conservatives. I preach to the choir because I want the choir to sing. So tonight I'm asking you to sing." Keynote address to the Goldwater Institute Annual Dinner, November 10, 2011. [31]

"I still think people elected me before in November 2010 and they'll elect me again because they want me to fix things. They want me to keep the focus and attention on fixing things. We're just going to make sure we've got a more comprehensive and inclusive process to get there . . . I'm not afraid to lose. I plan to win, I'm running to win, but I'm not afraid to lose to do the right thing." Speaking weeks before his 2012 recall election. [32]

I think the biggest thing goes beyond just November. It really goes to the heart of how people govern after the November elections. I think the message voters sent for Wisconsin, across the country and around the globe was voters are serious when they say they want their leaders to take on tough decisions and I think that is what was at stake.I think that people across America, certainly in my state, understand that America is at a tipping point and that we cannot sustain the kind of unprecedented growth we have right now in the national federal government. If [Mitt Romney] were to come in and talk specifically about how he is going to do this . . . The risk that he is willing to take to turn the country around, I think that would be compelling." Interview with CBS News' Dean Reynolds after winning his recall election. [33]

"[As I went up to the stage to declare victory], I just honed in on the three of them [his wife and two sons]. And I thought, 'Thank God, thank God, it's over for them.' The three of them had just gone through so much and they didn't ask for it. They didn't ask for the job. I did." Reacting after his victory in the 2012 recall election. [34]

"The mayor [Tom Barrett] could have had $50 million more, it wouldn't have made a difference. I think if you ask most voters today, everybody knew what was at stake. Everybody knew where I was, they knew what the mayor offered. There was no confusion. One of the positive things I looked at, this was one of those few elections where it wasn't based on some goofy sidebar issue. It wasn't based on some personality issue. It was fundamentally, here's where this side stands, here's where that side stands. Who do you pick? . . . [Now that the recall is over], we're not going to compromise our principles or anything like that. People shouldn't read this and say that nothing bold is ever going to happen again. But it's really a sense that people want to move on from this and we're really committed to doing that for everybody." After winning his 2012 recall election. [34]

"A wise governor told me a long time ago, political capital you don't get more of by keeping it. You get it by using it." [35]

"I'd like now and into the future to play a bigger role not only in Wisconsin and the Midwest, but nationally. I'd like to have an impact." [35]

"Certainly political capital-slash-celebrity attention, whatever you want to call it, certainly is part of the reason why I've been reaching out to CEOs. There's a lot of folks who probably would have taken a call from me before but are even more inclined now and are interested in what we're doing because of all the attention." [35]

"I don't think there's anybody who's going through anything tougher, so we can give some insights and lessons learned. There's things I'd do better. Those are lessons I'd love to pass onto anybody." [35]

SOURCES

Introduction

[1]. Theda Skocpol and Vanessa Williamson. *The Tea Party and the Remaking of Republican Conservatism*. New York: Oxford University Press, 2012, p. 168.

[2]. Theda Skocpol and Vanessa Williamson. *The Tea Party and the Remaking of Republican Conservatism*. New York: Oxford University Press, 2012, p. 192.

[3]. Eric Russell, "Maine Senate Republicans criticize LePage's comments, actions in upcoming OpEd," *Bangor Daily News*, April 1, 2011:
http://bangordailynews.com/2011/04/01/politics/senate-republicans-blast-lepage-comments-actions-in-op-ed/

[4]. Ann S. Kim, "State workers 'corrupted by bureaucracy," *Portland Press Herald*, April 28, 2012: http://www.pressherald.com/news/LePage-responds-to-critics-after-calling-state-workers-corrupt.html and Matthew Stone, "LePage says he didn't mean to offend with Gestapo comment; Republican leaders say it is 'non-issue,'" *Bangor Daily News*, July 9, 2012:
http://bangordailynews.com/2012/07/09/politics/republican-leaders-say-lepages-gestapo-comment-a-non-issue-accuse-dems-of-making-much-ado-about-nothing/

[5]. Lauren Sher, "CNBC's Santelli Rants About Housing Bailout," ABC News, February 19, 2009: http://abcnews.go.com/blogs/headlines/2009/02/cnbcs-santelli/

[6]. "Timeline: Rise of the Tea Party," CNN, November 2, 2010:
http://www.cnn.com/2010/POLITICS/11/02/timeline.tea.party/index.html

[7]. Alan Abramowitz. "Partisan Polarization and the Rise of the Tea Party Movement," Paper presented at the 2011 American Political Science Association Annual Meeting, Seattle; Morris P. Fiorina, Samuel J. Abrams, and Jeremy C. Pope. *Culture War? The Myth of a Polarized America*. 3rd ed. Longman, 2010; Matthew Levendusky, *The Partisan Sort: How Liberals Became Democrats and Conservatives Became Republicans*. 1st ed. University Of Chicago Press, 2009; and Geoffrey Kabaservice, *Rule and Ruin: The Downfall of Moderation and the Destruction of the Republican Party, From Eisenhower to the Tea Party*. Oxford University Press, USA, 2012.

[8]. Examples include David Lightman, "Santorum's appeal? He resonates with

angry Tea Party activists," McClatchy Newspapers, February 28, 2012: http://www.mcclatchydc.com/2012/02/28/140276/santorums-appeal-he-resonates.html and "Pining for Palin: What Most Conservatives Noticed," *MarkAmerica* blog, February 12, 2012: http://markamerica.com/2012/02/12/pining-for-palin-what-most-conservatives-noticed/

[9]. Susan Sharon, "LePage's Temperament Becomes Campaign Issue." MPBN.net, September 29, 2010: http://www.mpbn.net/Home/tabid/36/ctl/ViewItem/mid/3478/ItemId/13704/Default.aspx

Open for Business

Alaska: Interview with Sean Parnell, Governor of Alaska, *Travel Weekly*, March 22, 2010: http://www.travelweekly.com/In-the-Hot-Seat/Sean-Parnell,-Governor-of-Alaska/

Arizona: Michael Chihak interview with Arizona Governor Jan Brewer, February 18, 2011: http://www.azpm.org/news/story/2011/2/18/168-governor-touts-new-plan-arizona-is-open-for-business/

Florida: Aaron Deslatte, Jason Garcia, and Peter Franceschina, "Rick Scott, state's next governor, calls for Floridians to unite," *Orlando Sentinel*, November 2, 2010: http://articles.orlandosentinel.com/2010-11-03/news/os-florida-governor-election-results-20101103_1_rick-scott-democrat-alex-sink-lieutenant-governor

Idaho: Press release from Governor Otter encouraging Oregon businesses to move to Idaho to take advantage of lower taxes, March 8, 2010: http://gov.idaho.gov/mediacenter/press/pr2010/prmar10/pr_020.html

Kansas: Remarks during 2012 State of the State Address, "Kansas, State of Transition," January 11, 2012: http://media.kansas.com/smedia/2012/01/11/18/55/an6cB.So.80.pdf

Maine: "Radio Address: Maine is Open for Business," March 19, 2011: http://www.maine.gov/tools/whatsnew/index.php?topic=Gov_Radio_Addresses&id=216908&v=article and Kevin Miller, "LePage's 'Open for Business' sign disappears from I-95," *Bangor Daily News*, June 1, 2011: http://bangordailynews.com/2011/06/01/news/augusta/lepage%E2%80%99s-%E2%80%98open-for-business%E2%80%99-sign-stolen-off-i-95/ and Matt Wickenheiser, "LePage's 'Open for Business' Sign Replaced," *Bangor Daily News*, August 24, 2011: http://bangordailynews.com/2011/08/24/news/state/lepage%E2%80%99s-%E2%80%98open-for-business%E2%80%99-sign-replaced/

Michigan: "Q&A: Governor Rick Snyder," *Research Corridor*, April 4, 2011: http://researchcorridor.com/features/ricksnyderqa040411.aspx

New Mexico: Elaine Baumgartel, "N.M. Governor Susana Martinez Tough on Crime, Easy on Business," NPR, February 8, 2011: http://www.npr.org/2011/02/08/133563619/n-m-governor-tough-on-crime-easy-on-business

Ohio: "Kasich lobbies Chrysler, GM for new manufacturing jobs," Toledo Blade, January 13, 2011: http://www.toledoblade.com/Automotive/2011/01/13/Kasich-lobbies-Chrysler-GM-for-new-manufacturing-jobs.html

Pennsylvania: Katrina Wehr, "Corbett defeats Onorato," *Collegian Online*, November 3, 2010: http://www.collegian.psu.edu/archive/2010/11/03/governor_.aspx
South Carolina: Charleston Regional Business Report Staff Report, "Haley, House Republicans Take Aim at State's Labor Unions," Charleston Regional Business Journal, January 25, 2012: http://www.charlestonbusiness.com/news/42485-haley-house-republicans-take-aim-at-state-rsquo-s-labor-unions
Texas: 2010 Commercial featuring Rick Perry, "Texas Wide Open for Business." Available on You Tube:
http://www.youtube.com/watch?feature=player_embedded&v=XhO2HOtQsyA#!
Wisconsin: Press Release, January 12, 2011:
http://www.wisgov.state.wi.us/journal_media_detail.asp?prid=5569&locid=177

Jan Brewer

[1]. "Arizona's Brewer: Most Illegal Immigrants Are 'drug Mules,'" Cable News Network (CNN), June 27, 2010:
http://edition.cnn.com/2010/US/06/25/arizona.immigrants.drugs/?fbid=RzCBqp9fh10
[2]. Fox News, July 1, 2010, as cited in *USA Today*, "Quotes: Politicians and Officials Comment on Border Security," USATODAY.com, July 15, 2011:
http://www.usatoday.com/news/washington/2011-07-15-border-violence-quotes_n.html
[3]. Greta Van Susteren, "Gov. Brewer: 'We're on the Right Side of This Issue - I'm Going to Be Relentless!'" Fox News. FOX News Network, July 29, 2010:
http://www.foxnews.com/on-air/on-the-record/transcript/gov-brewer-039we039re-right-side-issue-i039m-going-be-relentless039
[4]. "Political insider: Brewer's media availability has been limited," *Arizona Republic*, June 10, 2011:
http://www.azcentral.com/news/election/azelections/articles/2011/07/10/20110710brewer-media-insider.html
[5]. Mike Sunnucks, "US wants 20-year ban on uranium mining near Grand Canyon," *Phoenix Business Journal*, June 20, 2011:
http://www.bizjournals.com/phoenix/news/2011/06/20/us-wants-20-year-ban-on-uranium-mining.html?ana=RSS
[6]. Christopher Palmieri, "Arizona's Brewer Prays Before Taking on Her Own Party on Taxes," *Bloomberg Businessweek*, May 24, 2011:
http://www.businessweek.com/news/2011-05-24/arizona-s-brewer-prays-before-taking-on-her-own-party-over-taxes.html -
[7]. "Gov. Brewer to Obama: Stop the Jokes, Secure the Border." *Fox News*, May 14, 2011: http://www.foxnews.com/politics/2011/05/14/gov-brewer-obama-stop-jokes-secure-border/
[8]. Alia Beard Rau, "Arizona immigration law affects legislative work," April 23, 2011. *Arizona Republic*:
http://www.azcentral.com/news/election/azelections/articles/2011/04/22/20110422sb1070-politics.html
[9]. Karina Bland, "Phoenix gay dads adopt, raise 12 happy kids," May 2, 2011. *Arizona Republic*:

http://www.azcentral.com/community/phoenix/articles/2011/05/02/20110502g
ay-dads-ham-family-12-adopted-kids.html

[10]. Responding to a lawsuit from the Freedom From Religion Foundation against
the law requiring the President to proclaim a National Day of Prayer. Donna Farris,
"National Day of Prayer is Constitutional." Suite101.com. April 28, 2011:
http://www.suite101.com/content/national-day-of-prayer-is-constitutional-
a368356

[11]. On questions about President Obama's birth certificate. Andrew Malcolm,
"Arizona Gov. Jan Brewer says 'birthers' are 'leading our country down a path of
destruction'" Top of the Ticket, *Los Angeles Times*, April 26, 2011:
http://latimesblogs.latimes.com/washington/2011/04/jan-brewer-thinks-birthers-
are-leading-our-country-down-a-path-of-destruction.html?utm_source=feedburner

[12]. Statement issued after signing bill into law banning abortions after 20 weeks.
Allison Yarrow, "Governor Jan Brewer Signs Arizona's Extreme New Abortion
Law," *Daily Beast*, April 12, 2012:
http://www.thedailybeast.com/articles/2012/04/12/governor-jan-brewer-signs-
arizona-s-extreme-new-abortion-law.html

[13.] On the budget problems she faced upon taking office and deciding to call for
a sales tax increase along with spending cuts. Daniel C. Vock, "Jan Brewer's
surprising tax fight," *Stateline* (Pew Center on the States), March 30, 2010:
http://www.stateline.org/live/details/story?contentId=473002

[14]. Interview on 12 News Sunday (KPNX-TV) with Brahm Resnik. Posted by
cpmaz. "12News' Sunday Square Off: Jan Brewer's "Let them eat cake" moment."
Random Musings, February 20, 2011:
http://cpmazrandommusings.blogspot.com/2011/02/12news-sunday-square-off-
jan-brewers.html

[15] Statement by Jan Brewer after signing a bill into law that bans the state or any
local government from using public money to contract with an organization that
includes abortions in its services-a proposal believed to be aimed in part at Planned
Parenthood. Sanchez, Yvonne Wingett. "Arizona Abortion-Services Bill Signed
into Law," *Arizona Republic*, May 4, 2012:
http://www.azcentral.com/arizonarepublic/local/articles/2012/05/04/20120504a
rizona-abortion-services-bill-signed-into-law.html

[16] Press release issued after signing a bill allowing "religiously affiliated"
employers to opt out of providing contraceptive coverage to their employees. Alia
Beard Rau, "Brewer signs Arizona bill on contraception coverage, *Arizona Republic*,
May 11 2012:
http://www.azcentral.com/news/articles/2012/05/11/20120511arizona-
contraception-bill-signed.html

Sam Brownback

[1]. John Gramlich, "In Kansas, Governor Sam Brownback drives a rightward
shift," *Stateline*, January 25, 2012:
http://stateline.org/live/details/story?contentId=627000

[2]. Brent D. Wistrom, "Brownback, others pray for guidance during legislative
session," *Wichita Eagle*, January 9, 2012 (updated January 26, 2012):
http://www.kansas.com/2012/01/09/2168849/brownback-others-pray-for-

guidance.html#storylink=cpy

[3]. Speaking at rally against the ACA contraception mandate at the Kansas State Capitol, Topeka, June 29, 2012. John Hanna (AP), "Kan,. Catholic bishops sponsor Statehouse rally," *SFGate.com,* June 29, 2012:

http://www.sfgate.com/news/article/Kan-Catholic-bishops-hold-Statehouse-rally-3672464.php

[4]. Rachel Whitten, "Brownback ushers in major anti-abortion laws," *Kansas Reporter,* April 12, 2011: http://www.kansasreporter.org/governor/73198.aspx

[5]. Tim Carpenter, "Brownback signs major abortion bills," *Topeka Capital-Journal,* April 12, 2011: http://cjonline.com/legislature/2011-04-12/brownback-signs-major-abortion-bills

[6]. Wesley Ernst, "Kansas Governor Signs Two Bills Limiting Abortion," *The Christian Post,* April 13, 2011: http://www.christianpost.com/news/kansas-governor-signs-two-bills-limiting-abortion-49813/

[7]. Manny Fernandez and Matt Flegenheimer, "100 Tornadoes in 24 Hours, But Plenty of Notice," *New York Times,* April 15, 2012:

http://www.nytimes.com/2012/04/16/us/violent-storms-cut-across-the-central-plains.html?_r=1

[8]. Speech at the University of Kansas, February 2, 2012. Vikaas Shanker, "Brownback speaks to students about human trafficking," *The University Daily Kansan,* February 2, 2012:

http://www.kansan.com/news/2012/feb/02/brownback-trafficking/

[9]. Speaking to reporters, June 28, 2012. John Hanna (AP), "Kansas gov.: Wait for November to act on health care," *Yahoo! Finance,* June 28, 2012:

http://finance.yahoo.com/news/kan-gov-wait-november-act-health-care-181532685-finance.html

[10]. Speech at Kansas Policy Institute, Wichita. Annie Gowen, "In Kansas, Gov. Sam Brownback puts tea party tenets into action with sharp cuts," *Washington Post,* December 21, 2011: http://www.washingtonpost.com/politics/in-kansas-gov-sam-brownback-puts-tea-party-tenets-into-action-with-sharp-cuts/2011/11/02/gIQAkbnOAP_story.html

[11]. Rachel Whitten, "Brownback signs voter ID into Kansas law," *Kansas Reporter,* April 18, 2011. http://www.kansasreporter.org/73361.aspx

[12]. John Milburn and Bill Draper (Associated Press), "Kansas gov. says staff overreacted to teen's tweet," *Boston Globe,* November 29, 2011:

http://www.boston.com/business/technology/articles/2011/11/29/kansas_gov_says_staff_overreacted_to_teens_tweet/?rss_id=Boston+Globe+-+Technology+stories

[13]. Associated Press, "Kansas dairy signs exclusive deal with Dannon", *Kansas City Star,* June 15, 2012:

http://www.kansascity.com/2012/06/15/3659830/kansas-dairy-signs-exclusive-deal.html

[14.] Praising the federal Production Tax Credit in a speech at the WindPower 2012 conference in Atlanta. Lindsay Morris, "The Big Question at WindPower 2012: What About the PTC?," *RenewableEnergyWorld.com,* June 4, 2012:

http://www.renewableenergyworld.com/rea/news/article/2012/06/the-big-question-at-windpower-2012-what-about-the-ptc?cmpid=rss

[15]. Steve Kraske and Brad Cooper, "Kansas governor's big agenda is off to slow start," *The Kansas City Star*, February 4, 2012: http://www.kansascity.com/2012/02/04/3410267/brownbacks-big-agenda-is-off-to.html#storylink=rss#storylink=cpy

[16]. Elizabeth Blair, "Kansas Cuts Funding for the Arts," NPR, June 23, 2011. See also Scott Rothschild, "Brownback's arts funding plan criticized as too little," *Lawrence Journal-World,* January 12, 2012: http://www2.ljworld.com/news/2012/jan/12/brownbacks-arts-funding-plan-criticized-too-little/

[17]. Calling for income tax cuts. John Milburn (AP), "Kan. lawmakers eye frenetic end to 2012 session," *The Hutchinson News,* April 24, 2012: http://www.hutchnews.com/Localregional/BC-KS-XGR-Session-Resumes-3rd-Ld-Writethr-20120424-20-19-49

[18]. Interview with *Kansas Reporter*. Gene Meyer, "Kansas Gov. says continued cost cutting key to tax changes," *Kansas Reporter*, no date given (circa December 2011): http://www.kansasreporter.org/governor/85641.aspx

[19]. Speaking at a Wyandotte County, Kansas site where a Missouri business is building a new facility. Amy Hawley, "Critics: KS income tax cuts come with a catch," KSHB-TV (NBC affiliate, Kansas City), April 30, 2012: http://www.kshb.com/dpp/news/state/kansas/critics-ks-income-tax-cuts-come-with-a-catch

[20]. Associated Press, "Poor face tax increase under Brownback plan, new state figures show," *Wichita Eagle,* January 12, 2012: http://www.kansas.com/2012/01/17/2178691/poor-face-tax-increase-under-brownbacks.html#storylink=cpy

[21]. Laying out his vision for Kansas in his State of the State Address, January 11, 2012. Russ Morgan, "Local Lawmakers Respond to Brownback Speech," *Emporia Gazette*, January 12, 2012: http://www.emporiagazette.com/news/2012/jan/12/local-lawmakers-respond-brownback-speech/

[22]. May 31, 2012, upon signing the new state budget. Paul Koepp, "Brownback signs $14B budget, vetoes some items," *Kansas City Business Journal*, June 1, 2012: http://www.bizjournals.com/kansascity/news/2012/06/01/brownback-signs-14b-kansas-budget.html?ana=RSS&s=article_search&utm_source=feedburner&utm_medium=feed&utm_campaign=Feed%3A+bizj_kansascity+%28Kansas+City+Business+Journal%29

[23]. Scott Rothschild, "Brownback plans to sign more aggressive tax-cutting bill after Senate halts alternative," LJWorld.com, May 18, 2012: http://www2.ljworld.com/news/2012/may/18/brownback-plans-sign-more-aggressive-tax-cutting-b/

[24]. Interview with the *Kansas Reporter*, December 21, 2011. Gene Meyer and Rachel Whitten, "Brownback lays out budget priorities,*" Kansas Reporter*, December 22, 2011: http://www.kansasreporter.org/governor/69769.aspx

[25]. State Capitol, May 4, 2012. Brad Cooper, "Brownback seems lukewarm on Senate education plan," *Kansas City Star*'s *Midwest Democracy* blog, May 4, 2012: http://midwestdemocracy.com/articles/brownback-not-excited-about-senate-

education-plan/#storylink=rss#storylink=cpy

[26]. Press release, "Gov. Brownback: Stopping ObamaCare in Hands of American People," Posted on Brownback's Facebook page, June 28, 2012: https://www.facebook.com/notes/governor-sam-brownback/gov-brownback-stopping-obamacare-in-hands-of-american-people/389901391059431

[27]. Sam Brownback press release, "Gov.-Elect Names Secretary of Administration Nominee," December 16, 2010. Reprinted in *The Kansas Progress*, circa December 16, 2010: http://www.kansasprogress.com/wordpress/index.php/2010/12/16/governor-elect-sam-brownback-attorney-dennis-taylor-as-his-nominee-for-secretary-of-administration/

[28]. Rebecca Kaplan, "Brownback Won't Endorse in Kansas Caucuses," *National Journal*, March 10, 2012: http://www.nationaljournal.com/2012-presidential-campaign/brownback-won-t-endorse-in-kansas-caucuses-20120309

[29]. Press release, "Governor Brownback Issues Independence Day Message." July 4, 2012," Posted on KMAN-AM (Manhattan, KS) website: http://1350kman.com/?p=17800

[30]. Editorial, "The Heartland Tax Rebellion," *Wall Street Journal*, February 8, 2012: http://online.wsj.com/article/SB10001424052970203889904577200872159113492.html

Chris Christie

[1]. "Christie Slams N.J. Teacher Union, Calls for Ed. Reform," CBS 2 (New York), September 7, 2011: http://newyork.cbslocal.com/2010/09/07/christie-lashes-out-at-n-j-teacher-union-call-for-ed-reform/

[2]. "Remarks of Governor Chris Christie to the Special session of the New Jersey Legislature Regarding the Budget for Fiscal Year 2010," February 11, 2010: http://www.state.nj.us/governor/news/addresses/2010s/approved/20100211.html

[3]. Richard Perez-Pena, "Christie Hopes to Lure Businesses Fleeing Illinois Taxes," *New York Times*, January 13, 2011: http://www.nytimes.com/2011/01/14/nyregion/14illinois.html?_r=1&partner=rss&emc=rss

[4]. Eric W. Dolan, "New Jersey Gov. Christie: Let schools teach creationism," *Raw Story*, May 15, 2011: http://www.rawstory.com/rs/2011/05/15/new-jersey-gov-christie-let-schools-teach-creationism/

[5]. Cindy Long, "Teacher Pay Still Losing Ground," *NEA Today*, April 5, 2011: http://neatoday.org/2011/04/05/teacher-pay-losing-ground/

[6]. Claire Heininger, "Gov. Chris Christie accuses N.J. teachers' union of 'using students like drug mules' in school elections," NJ.com, April 19, 2010: http://www.nj.com/news/index.ssf/2010/04/gov_chris_christie_accuses_nj.html

[7] James Freeman, "New Jersey's 'Failed Experiment'" (interview with New Jersey Governor Chris Christie), *The Wall Street Journal*, April 17, 2010: http://online.wsj.com/article/SB10001424052702303348504575184120546772244.html

[8]. Interview with Neil Cavuto, "Gov. Chris Christie on McChrystal's Downfall, Battle With Teachers' Unions," *Your World: Cavuto*, Fox News, June 23, 2010:

http://www.foxnews.com/on-air/your-world-cavuto/transcript/gov-chris-christie-mcchrystals-downfall-battle-teachers-unions#ixzz1T8ErhX6E

[9] Natasha Lennard, "Chris Christie calls fears over Muslim judge 'crap,'" *Salon*, August 4, 2011: http://www.salon.com/news/politics/war_room/2011/08/04/christie_defends_muslim_judge

[10] Adam Serwer, "Chris Christie smacks down the sharia crowd," The Plum Line (blog), *Washington Post*, August 4, 2011: http://www.washingtonpost.com/blogs/plum-line/post/chris-christie-smacks-down-the-sharia-crowd/2011/03/04/gIQARsBBuI_blog.html

[11]. Interview with Sean Hannity on "Hannity," Fox News Channel, January 19, 2012: http://www.foxnews.com/on-air/hannity/2012/01/20/gov-christie-staging-new-jersey-comeback#ixzz1k7OdDYoG

[12] Speech, "It's Time to do the Big Things," to the American Enterprise Institute, Washington , D. C., February 16, 2011: http://www.aei.org/events/2011/02/16/its-time-to-do-the-big-things-event/

[13] Tim Mak, "Chris Christie tells Warren Buffett: 'Shut up,'" *Politico*, February 22, 2012: http://www.politico.com/news/stories/0212/73155.html#ixzz1nLr0T7j9

[14]. MJ Lee, "Christie calls Democrat 'numb nuts,'" *Fox Nation*, January 30, 2012: http://nation.foxnews.com/chris-christie/2012/01/31/christie-calls-democrat-numb-nuts

[15] Maggie Haberman, "Christie to protesters: Jobs not going down, sweetheart." *Politico*, January 8, 2012: http://www.politico.com/blogs/burns-haberman/2012/01/christie-to-protesters-jobs-not-going-down-sweetheart-110112.html

[16]. Marcia Kramer, "Christie's 'None of Your Business' Comment Ruffles Feathers of N.J. Voters," *CBS New York,* June 17, 2011: http://newyork.cbslocal.com/2011/06/17/christies-its-none-of-your-business-comment-ruffles-feathers-of-n-j-voters/

[17]. *Fox News Insider*, "QUOTE OF THE DAY: Gov. Chris Christie Tells NJ Residents to 'Get the Hell Off the Beach' as Irene Approaches," August 26, 2011: http://foxnewsinsider.com/2011/08/26/quote-of-the-day-gov-chris-christie-tells-nj-residents-to-get-the-hell-off-the-beach-as-irene-approaches/

[18]. MJ Lee, "Chris Christie: President Obama's just a 'bystander,'" *Politico*, November 29, 2011: http://www.politico.com/news/stories/1111/69280.html#ixzz1nM1VzPQC

[19]. Chris Megerian, *NJ.com*, "Gov. Christie says he didn't object to firing of Quran-burning NJ Transit worker," February 15, 2011: http://www.nj.com/news/index.ssf/2011/02/gov_christie_says_he_didnt_obj.html

[20]. UPI, "YouTube child is governor for a day," *UPI.com*, April 6, 2011: http://www.upi.com/Odd_News/2011/04/06/YouTube-child-is-NJ-governor-for-a-day/UPI-62191302126140/

[21]. Jenna Portnoy, "Gov. Christie tells Oprah he'll be 'much more ready' in 2016, *NJ.com,* January 15, 2012: http://www.nj.com/news/index.ssf/2012/01/gov_christie_tells_oprah_hell.html

[22]. "In honor of Whitney Houston, Gov. Christie ordering flags flown at half-

staff in N.J.", *NJ.com*, February 14, 2012:
http://www.nj.com/news/index.ssf/2012/02/whitney_houston_flags_half-sta.html

[23] CBS/Associated Press, "Whitney Houston: N.J. Governor defends lowering flags for singer," *CBSNews.com*, February 16, 2012:
http://www.cbsnews.com/8301-31749_162-57379123-10391698/whitney-houston-n.j-governor-defends-lowering-flags-for-singer/

[24]. Max Pizarro, "Governor proposes tax relief for everyone: 10% across the board; in conjunction with education overhaul," *Politicker NJ*, January 12, 2011:
http://www.politickernj.com/54006/governor-proposes-tax-relief-everyone

[25]. Salvador Rizzo, "Gov. Christie proposes 10 percent N.J. tax reduction," *NJ.com*, January 17, 2012:
http://www.nj.com/news/index.ssf/2012/01/gov_christie_proposes_10_perce.html

[26]. Megan DeMarco, "Democrats propose to restore aid to distressed N. J. cities," *NorthJersey.com*, November 28, 2011:
http://www.northjersey.com/news/politics/112811_Democrats_propose_to_restore_aid_for_distressed_NJ_cities.html

[27]. Christopher Baxter, "Gov. Christie: Let's offer non-violent drug offenders treatment, not prison," NorthJersey.com, November 28, 2011:
http://www.northjersey.com/news/state/Christie_to_give_plans_for_prisoner_re-entry.html

[28]. Robin Rieger, "Christie: No Regret for 'Idiot' Remark," *CBS Philly*, March 12, 2012: http://philadelphia.cbslocal.com/2012/03/12/christie-no-regret-for-idiot-remark/and Fox & Friends, "Governor Chris Christie Doesn't Hold Back, Calls Law Student an 'Idiot' For Heckling," *Fox News Insider,* March 10, 2012:
http://foxnewsinsider.com/2012/03/10/governor-chris-christie-doesnt-hold-back-calling-law-student-an-idiot-for-heckling/

[29]. Salvador Rizzo, "Gov. Christie calls Gingrich 'an embarrassment to his party'," *NJ.com*, January 23, 2012:
http://www.nj.com/news/index.ssf/2012/01/gov_christie_calls_gingrich_an.html

[30]. Megan DeMarco, "Gov. Christie Calls Lautenberg 'a partisan hack' for his criticism of proposed Rutgers-Rowan merger," *NJ.Com* , March 29, 2012:
http://www.nj.com/news/index.ssf/2012/03/gov_christie_calls_sen_lautenb.html#incart_mce

[31] "Gov. Christie calls made-to-order bills report 'totally ridiculous,'" *NJ.com*, April 3, 2012:
http://www.nj.com/news/index.ssf/2012/04/gov_christie_calls_made-to-ord.html#incart_hbx

[32]. Speech at a tax policy conference sponsored by the President George W. Bush Institute, New York City, April 10, 2012. Tom Moran, "Gov. Chris Christie's condescending speech out of touch with Americans' reality," *NJ.com*, April 12, 2012:
http://blog.nj.com/njv_tom_moran/2012/04/gov_chris_christies_condescend.html and Megan DeMarco, "Gov. Christie: Nation turning into people sitting on a couch waiting for their next government check," *NJ.com*, April 10, 2012:
http://www.nj.com/news/index.ssf/2012/04/gov_christie_nation_is_becomin.ht

ml

[33]. John Reitmeyer, "N.J. Gov. Christie: Abortion an issue 'whose time has come,'" North Jersey.com, January 24, 2011:
http://www.northjersey.com/news/national/012411_NJ_Gov_Chris_Christie_to_speak_at_anti-abortion_rally_in_Trenton.html?c=y&page=2

[34]. Ben Golliver, "New Jersey Governor on Nets moving to Brooklyn: 'Good riddance,'" *Eye on Basketball* blog (CBS Sports), April 23, 2012:
http://www.cbssports.com/nba/blog/eye-on-basketball/18793846/new-jersey-governor-on-nets-move-to-brooklyn-good-riddance

[35]. Bill Glauber, Mike Johnson and Meg Jones, "N.J. governor stumps for Walker around state," *Milwaukee Journal Sentinel,* May 1, 2012:
http://www.jsonline.com/news/statepolitics/nj-governor-stumps-for-walker-around-state-tc58cbn-149761415.html

[36]. David Edwards, "New Jersey Gov. Says He Wants to "Take the Bat" to a 76-year Old Widow," *The Raw Story.com,* April 14, 2011:
http://www.rawstory.com/rs/2011/04/14/new-jersey-gov-says-he-wants-to-take-the-bat-to-a-76-year-old-widow/

[37]. Alex Becker, "Chris Christie Calls War on Drugs 'A Failure,'" *Huffington Post,* July 10, 2012: http://www.huffingtonpost.com/2012/07/09/chris-christie-drugs-war-on-drugs_n_1659687.html

[38]. Tim Mak, "Chris Christie: health care was 'extortion,'" *Politico,* July 10, 2012: http://www.politico.com/news/stories/0712/78324.html

[39]. "Gov. Christie calls reporter 'idiot' for asking off-topic question at news conference," *Newark Star Ledger,* June 30, 2012:
http://www.nj.com/news/index.ssf/2012/06/gov_christie_asks_if_reporter.html

[40]. Jeffrey Goldberg, "Jersey Boys," *The Atlantic,* July/August 2012:
http://www.theatlantic.com/magazine/archive/2012/07/jersey-boys/9019/

Tom Corbett

[1]. Interview with Scott Detrow. Arthur Delaney, "Tom Corbett Says The Unemployed Just 'Sit There,'" *Huffington Post,* July 13, 2010:
http://www.huffingtonpost.com/2010/07/13/tom-corbett-says-the-unem_n_644379.html

[2] Laura Bonatis, "No Lucky Charms in Corbett's Budget", *Politics PA,* March 18, 2011: http://www.politicspa.com/protesters-no-lucky-charms-in-corbett%E2%80%99s-budget/22573/

[3]. Text of Governor Corbett's budget address, March 8, 2011. Reprinted at http://articles.philly.com/2011-03-08/news/28668900_1_budget-address-first-budget-tree

[4]. Statement following Supreme Court ruling on the Affordable Care Act. Chris Mondics, "Supreme Court upholds health-care overhaul," *Philadelphia Inquirer,* June 29, 2012:
http://www.philly.com/philly/health/20120629_Supreme_Court_upholds_health-care_overhaul.html

[5]. Speaking at the dedication of the Flight 93 National Memorial, Stonycreek, PA, September 11, 2011. Mackenzie Carpenter, Ann Rodgers, Bill Toland, and Sean Hamill, "President lays wreath at Flight 93 memorial," *Pittsburgh Post-Gazette,*

September 11, 2011: http://old.post-gazette.com/pg/11254/1173963-100.stm

[6]. Interview on "Fox News Sunday," Nov. 12, 2011. UPI, "Pa. governor lost faith in Paterno," November 13, 2011:
http://www.upi.com/Top_News/US/2011/11/13/Pa-governor-lost-confidence-in-Paterno/UPI-63411321207121/

[7]. B.A. Birch, 'Pennsylvania Gov. Tom Corbett Talks About Voucher Plan," *Education News*, October 11, 2011: http://www.educationnews.org/education-policy-and-politics/pennsylvania-gov-tom-corbett-speaks-about-voucher-plan/

[8]. Speaking at Lincoln Charter School in York, PA, October 11, 2011. Marc Levy, "Corbett Touts School Vouchers in Education Agenda," *Philadelphia Tribune*, October 11, 2011.: http://www.phillytrib.com/newsarticles/item/996-corbett-touts-school-vouchers-in-education-agenda.html

[9]. Brian O'Neill, "Budget hurts, but gas drillers feel no pain," *Pittsburgh Post-Gazette*, March 10, 2011: http://old.post-gazette.com/pg/11069/1130934-155.stm

[10]. Gubernatorial press release, February 13, 2012:
http://www.newpa.com/newsroom/governor-corbett-signs-historic-marcellus-shale-law

[11]. Addressing a joint session of the Pa. legislature. John L. Micek and Steve Esack, "Corbett's no-tax increase budget hikes public school funds, slashes higher ed spending," *The Morning Call*, February 7, 2012: http://articles.mcall.com/2012-02-07/news/mc-pa-corbett-budget-speech-20120207_1_spending-plan-tom-corbett-higher-education

[12]. Speaking at a waterways conference in Pittsburgh, Fall 2011. *Waterway News*," GOVERNOR ADVOCATES IMPORTANCE OF RIVERS," *Waterway News*, November 2, 2011:
http://www.waterwaynews.com/ARCHIVE/2011%20NOVEMBER/2011%20NOVEMBER%2002/2011%20NOVEMBER%2002%20GOVERNOR%20IS%20ADVOCATE%20OF%20IMPORTANCE%20OF%20RIVERS.html

[13]. 2011 State of the State address. Excerpted in OnTheIssues.com, "Tom Corbett on Tax Reform":
http://ontheissues.org/Governor/Tom_Corbett_Tax_Reform.htm

[14]. 2012 budget address. Monica Yant Kinney, 'Corbett won't dare mention the mentally disabled," *Philadelphia Inquirer*, February 8, 2012:
http://www.philly.com/philly/columnists/monica_yant_kinney/20120208_Monica_Yant_Kinney__Corbett_won_t_dare_mention_the_mentally_disabled.html

[15.] Angela Couloumbis and Amy Worden, "Corbett says he would sign voter-ID bill," *Philadelphia Inquirer*, March 13, 2012: http://articles.philly.com/2012-03-13/news/31160167_1_voter-id-bill-voter-id-evidence-of-voter-fraud

[16]. UPI, "Pa. adopts voter ID law," UPI.com, March 15, 2012:
http://www.upi.com/Top_News/US/2012/03/15/Pa-adopts-voter-ID-law/UPI-18531331788052/#ixzz1r0OgorOj

[17]. Inaugural address, January 18, 2011. Reprinted at:
http://www.philly.com/philly/blogs/cityhall/Gov_Corbett_Calls_For_Civility_In_Public_Debate.html

[18]. Madeleine Dean, "Pennsylvanians, you just have to 'close your eyes,'" *PhillyBurbs.com*, March 23, 2012:
http://www.phillyburbs.com/news/local/the_intelligencer_news/opinion/pennsyl

vanians-you-just-have-to-close-your-eyes/article_75677ef8-e3c4-5e6d-9cb6-603dc3a11ca3.html

Nikki Haley

[1]. From Haley's 2012 autobiography, *Can't is Not An Option: My American Story* cited in Cristina Merrill, "Nikki Haley Book: South Carolina Governor Talks Dirty Politics, Tea Party in 'Can't Is Not An Option,'" *International Business Times*, April 12, 2012: http://www.ibtimes.com/articles/327443/20120412/nikki-haley-book-south-carolina-governor-tea.htm

[2]. The Pajama Pundit, Quote of the Day: Nikki Haley edition, May 17, 2011: http://www.thepajamapundit.com/2011/05/quote-of-day-nikki-haley-edition.html

[3]. After the June 201 South Carolina gubernatorial primary. UPI, "South Carolinians get runoff for gov.," June 9, 2010: http://www.upi.com/Top_News/US/2010/06/09/South-Carolinians-get-GOP-runoff-for-gov/UPI-84801276060210/

[4]. Interview with Fox Carolina in which she responded to complaints that the new Voter ID law was discriminatory. Chris Haire, "Nikki Haley wants to drive you to the DMV," *Charleston City Paper*, July 14, 2011: http://www.charlestoncitypaper.com/HaireoftheDog/archives/2011/07/14/nikki-haley-wants-to-drive-you-to-the-dmv

[5]. Interview with Fox Carolina in which she responded to complaints that the new law was discriminatory. Chris Haire, "Nikki Haley wants to drive you to the DMV," *Charleston City Paper*, July 14, 2011: http://www.charlestoncitypaper.com/HaireoftheDog/archives/2011/07/14/nikki-haley-wants-to-drive-you-to-the-dmv

[6]. *The Times and Democrat*, "Rural Summit Honors Walterboro Effort," *TheTandD.com*, March 14, 2012: http://thetandd.com/business/rural-summit-honors-walterboro-effort/article_69d5b11a-6a48-11e1-915f-0019bb2963f4.html#ixzz1qFG1uhZg

[7]. Tony Santaella, "Original Six Foundation to Create 'Allendale County Day', WLTX.com, March 7, 2012: http://www.wltx.com/rss/article/177675/2/Original-Six-to-Create-Allendale-County-Day

[8]. Alexis Levinson, "Republican governors: Obama is all talk, no action," *The Daily Caller*, February 27, 2012: http://dailycaller.com/2012/02/27/republican-governors-obama-is-all-talk-no-action/

[9]. Quin Hilyer, "More on Common Core (Nationalized Education: Yuck)," *Freedom Line* Blog, February 28, 2012: http://cfif.org/v/freedom_line_blog/13185/more-on-common-core-nationalized-education-yuck/

[10]. Facebook post, May 27, 2012. https://www.facebook.com/NikkiHaley (NOTE: All other posts from Haley's Facebook page have this same URL.)

[11]. Statement after the final 2012 Republican presidential candidate debate in South Carolina. *The Asian Age*, "US can't afford Obama as president for 4 more yrs: Haley," *The Asian Age*, January 17, 2012: http://www.asianage.com/international/us-cant-afford-obama-president-4-more-yrs-haley-120

[12]. From Haley's 2012 autobiography, *Can't is Not An Option: My American Story* cited in Cristina Merrill, "Nikki Haley Book: South Carolina Governor Talks Dirty Politics, Tea Party in 'Can't Is Not An Option,'" *International Business Times*, April 12, 2012: http://www.ibtimes.com/articles/327443/20120412/nikki-haley-book-south-carolina-governor-tea.htm

[13]. Facebook post, August 26, 2011.

[14]. Facebook post, November 29, 2011.

[15]. Facebook post, May 23, 2012.

[16]. Speaking outside of Banks Construction Company in North Charleston, SC. Paul Bowers, "Haley pitches tax cuts in North Charleston," *Charleston City Paper*, March 14, 2012: http://www.charlestoncitypaper.com/charleston/haley-pitches-tax-cuts-in-north-charleston/Content?oid=4038635

[17]. Facebook post, June 28, 2012.

[18]. Josh McCann, "Tanger Outlet Center 1: They came, they shopped, they exalted," *The Island Packet*, March 31, 2011: http://www.islandpacket.com/2011/03/31/1603744/tanger-outlet-center-1-they-came.html

[19]. Rocky Dohmen, "Haley announces stance on 'Obamacare' via Facebook," *The Digitel Myrtle Beach*, July 2, 2012: http://myrtlebeach.thedigitel.com/politics/haley-announces-obamacare-stance-facebook-36696-0702

[20]. Introducing Mitt Romney at a Romney campaign rally in Columbia, SC, January 11, 2012. Michael Falcone, "Are Romney's Foes Backing Off Bain,?" *The Note* blog (ABC News), January 12, 2012: http://abcnews.go.com/blogs/politics/2012/01/are-romneys-foes-backing-off-bain-the-note/

[21]. Speaking outside the South Carolina capitol introducing Sarah Palin, 2010. Page 139 in Haley's autobiography *Can't is Not an Option: My American Story* (2012).

[22]. Speaking to a South Carolina Association of Taxpayers gathering, March 7, 2012. Adam Beam, "Haley criticizes House budget for not including tax relief", *Myrtle Beach Online*, March 7, 2012: http://www.myrtlebeachonline.com/2012/03/07/2702762/haley-criticizes-house-budget.html#storylink=cpy

[23]. Facebook post, March 29, 2012: https://www.facebook.com/NikkiHaley/posts/10150641848673226

[24]. Nikki Haley for Governor website, http://www.nikkihaley.com/truthinfacts

[25]. 2012 State of the State speech. Excerpts taken from James T. Hammond, "Haley calls for lower taxes, tort reform," *Charleston Regional Business Journal*, January 19, 2012: http://www.charlestonbusiness.com/news/42413/print

[26]. Speaking about and on behalf of Scott Walker at a printing plant in Sussex, Wisconsin, June 1, 2012. CBS/Associated Press, "Big guns stump in Wis. as recall election nears," CBS This Morning, June 2, 2012: http://www.cbsnews.com/8301-505263_162-57446062/big-guns-stump-in-wis-as-recall-election-nears/

[27]. Facebook post, June 7, 2012.

[28]. Facebook post shortly after taking office, January 16, 2011.

[29]. Facebook post, October 9, 2011.

[30]. Facebook post, November 11, 2011.

[31]. Facebook post, November 16, 2011.

[32]. Facebook post, July 2, 2012 (capitals in the original).

[33]. Introducing Senator Marco Rubio at a Republican fundraising dinner in Columbia, SC, May 19, 2012. Corey Hutchins, "VIDEO: Outgoing S.C. Union Leader Smashes Nikki Haley Piñata with Bat," Columbia 9SC) *Free Times*, May 22, 2012: http://www.free-times.com/index.php?cat=1992209084141467&act=post&pid=11862205124358729

[34]. Speaking before the South Carolina House Ethics Committee, June 28, 2012. Note: The charges against her were dismissed. Tim Smith, "Haley calls accuser 'racist, sexist bigot,'" *GreenvilleOnline.com*, June 29, 2012: http://www.greenvilleonline.com/article/20120629/NEWS03/306290008/Haley-calls-accuser-racist-sexist-bigot-?nclick_check=1

[35]. Interview with Greta Van Susteren on "On The Record With Greta Van Susteren," Fox News Channel, May 23, 2012: http://www.foxnews.com/on-air/on-the-record/2012/05/24/decency-takes-beating-along-nikki-haley-pinata?page=2

[36]. Fundraising letter sent to supporters reprinted in *Fitsnews* blog, "Nikki Haley Uses Piñata Incident To Raise Money," May 23, 2012: http://www.fitsnews.com/2012/05/23/nikki-haley-uses-pinata-incident-to-raise-money/

[37]. Statement at a press conference, December 8, 2010. John McDermott, "Union's lawsuit tossed; Judge rules remarks by Haley, official free speech," *The Post and Courier*, August 9, 2011 (updated March 23, 2012): http://www.postandcourier.com/apps/pbcs.dll/article?AID=/20110809/PC04/308099926&template=printart

[38]. John Nichols, "Scott Walker's Southern Strategy Aligns Him With 'Union Buster' Nikki Haley," *The Nation*, May 14, 2012: http://www.thenation.com/blog/168052/scott-walkers-southern-strategy-aligns-him-union-buster-nikki-haley#

[39]. Facebook posting, March 2012. The Digitel Myrtle Beach Staff Reports, "South Carolina continues the gambling discussion: Update: Steve Porter Editorial," *The Digitel Myrtle Beach*, April 8, 2012: http://myrtlebeach.thedigitel.com/freestyle/myrtlebeach-casino-34308-0121

[40]. Appearing on ABC-TV's "The View," April 3, 2012. David Edwards, "Nikki Haley: 'Women don't care about contraception,'" *The Raw Story*, April 3, 2012: http://www.rawstory.com/rs/2012/04/03/nikki-haley-women-dont-care-about-contraception/

[41]. Interview with ABC-TV's Christine Amanpour, May 2011. Jessica Desvarieux, "Nikki Haley Says Health Care Will Remain Issue For Romney," *ABC News*, May 15, 2011: http://abcnews.go.com/Politics/nikki-haley-health-care-remain-issue-romney/story?id=13606953

[42]. Facebook post, November 6, 2011.

[43]. 2010 campaign video posted on YouTube; cited by Sarah Jaffe, "Nikki Haley: A New Face for Old Politics in South Carolina," *The Nation*, November 1, 2010: http://www.thenation.com/article/155730/nikki-haley-new-face-old-politics-south-carolina#

[44]. Facebook post, June 29, 2012:

https://www.facebook.com/NikkiHaley/posts/10150918469013226

[45]. Facebook post explaining her veto of funding for the state Arts Commission, July 7, 2012.

[46]. Facebook post, June 11, 2012.

[47]. Facebook post, May 27, 2011.

[48]. Facebook post, August 13, 2011.

[49]. 2012 State of the State Address. Erin McKee, "Note to Nikki: Unions do have a role in S. C.," *The Post and Courier*, January 27, 2012:
http://www.postandcourier.com/article/20120127/ARCHIVES/301279935

John Kasich

[1]. Speech in January 2011. Reginald Fields, "Gov. John Kasich calls police officer 'idiot,'" Cleveland *Plain Dealer*, February 16, 2011:
http://www.cleveland.com/open/index.ssf/2011/02/ohio_gov_john_kasich_calls
_pol.html

[2]. Appearing on the Sean Hannity show, Fox News Channel, July 8, 2009. Brad Johnson, "GOP Governor Candidates Oppose Clean Energy Jobs," *Think Progress.org*, October 13, 2010: http://thinkprogress.org/report/gop-governor-deniers/

[3]. 2011 State of the State Address, Ohio Statehouse, Columbus:
http://media.cleveland.com/pdextra/other/State-of-th-state.pdf

[4]. Interview on CNN with Jessica Yellin, February 21, 2011. John King, "Interview with John Kasich," *Real Clear Politics*:
http://www.realclearpolitics.com/articles/2011/02/21/interview_with_ohio_gove
rnor_john_kasich_108988.html

[5]. Juliet Williams (Associated Press), "Bitter debate over debt ceiling reflects partisan divide in states struggling with budget gaps," *Yahoo! Canada Finance*, August 7, 2011: http://ca.finance.yahoo.com/news/Bitter-debate-debt-ceiling-capress-2713624134.html?x=0

[6]. Speech at the Ashtabula County Lincoln Day Breakfast, Ashtabula, Ohio, March 2009. Carl E. Feather, "Kasich promises county won't be forgotten if Republicans regain control," *The Star Beacon* (Ashtabula), March 24, 2009:
http://starbeacon.com/local/x343701395/Kasich-promises-county-won-t-be-forgotten-if-Republicans-regain-control/print

[7]. Discussing a reform plan for the Cleveland public schools at a luncheon speech in Cleveland, March 15, 2012. Karen Farkas, "Cleveland Mayor Frank Jackson's school bill a worry for Gov. John Kasich," Cleveland *Plain Dealer*, March 16, 2012:
http://blog.cleveland.com/metro/2012/03/governor_kasich_wants_legislat.html

[8]. Stephanie Banchero, "Cleveland Cooperates on School Overhaul," *Wall Street Journal*, July 10, 2012.

[9]. *News-Herald* staff, "Editorial: State smart to alter method of grading," *The News-Herald*, March 25, 2012: http://www.news-herald.com/articles/2012/03/25/opinion/nh5270682.txt?viewmode=fullstory

[10]. Pat Holmes and Deanna Pan, "Death toll drops in drug war," *Columbus Dispatch*, April 1, 2012:
http://www.dispatch.com/content/stories/local/2012/04/01/death-toll-drops-in-drug-war.html

[11]. Speech to the Columbus Metropolitan Club, July 29, 2011. Denise Yost, "Kasich Talks Goals For Future; Says State Full Of 'Whackadoodles,'" *Ohio Votes 2011*, July 29, 2011: http://www2.ohiovotes2011.com/news/2011/jul/29/kasich-talks-goals-future-says-state-filled-whacka-ar-648351/

[12]. Reginald Fields, "John Kasich, Yvette McGee Brown differ on rail plan at candidate forum," Cleveland *Plain Dealer*, August 4, 2010: http://www.cleveland.com/open/index.ssf/2010/08/john_kasich_yvette_mcgee_brown.html

[13]. Jeanine Kendle, "Quote-worthy this week," Wooster *Daily Record*, January 16, 2011.

[14]. Associated Press, "Gov. Kasich signs sweeping $56B Ohio Budget," *Canton Repository*, June 30, 2011: http://www.cantonrep.com/ohio/x1722635240/Gov-Kasich-signs-sweeping-56B-Ohio-budget

[15]. Jeff Bell, "Passenger rail proponents a 'train cult,'" Columbuz Biz Insider Blog, *Columbus Business First*, December 2, 2010: http://www.bizjournals.com/columbus/blog/2010/12/kasich-passenger-rail-proponents-a.html

[16]. Joe Vardon, "Kasich won't take 'no' for an answer," *Columbus Dispatch*, March 19, 2012: http://www.dispatch.com/content/stories/local/2012/03/19/kasich-wont-take-no-for-an-answer.html

[17]. Speaking at a Ross County, Ohio Republican function, April 5, 2012. Joe Vardon, "Kasich breaks ranks, speaks of climate change," *Columbus Dispatch*, April 10, 2012: http://www.dispatch.com/content/stories/local/2012/04/10/kasich-speaks-of-climate-change.html

[18]. Comments on "Morning Joe," MSNBC, July 12, 2011. Kyle Cheney, "National GOP sees Mass. bargaining law as wedge against Pres. Obama," *Boston Herald*, July 14, 2011: http://www.bostonherald.com/news/politics/view.bg?articleid=1351772&srvc=rss&utm_source=feedburner&utm_medium=feed&utm_campaign=Feed%3A+bostonherald%2Fnews+%28News+%26+Opinion+-+BostonHerald.com%29

[19]. Laura A. Bischoff, "Kasich defends Cabinet despite diversity dispute," *Dayton Daily News*, February 6, 2011: http://www.daytondailynews.com/news/kasich-defends-cabinet-despite-diversity-dispute-1073920.html

[20]. January 17, 2012. Joe Vardon, "In emotional speech, Kasich talks of faith, civil rights," *Columbus Dispatch*, January 18, 2012: http://www.dispatch.com/content/stories/local/2012/01/18/in-emotional-speech-kasich-talks-of-faith-civil-rights.html

[21]. Columbus, March 29, 2012. Jim Provance, "Kasich targets human trafficking", *Toledo Blade*, March 30, 2012: http://www.toledoblade.com/State/2012/03/30/Kasich-targets-human-trafficking.html

[22]. June 27, 2012. Rob Wiercinski, "Kasich signs human trafficking bill in Toledo," *Toledo News Now* (WTOL-TV), June 27, 2012: http://www.toledonewsnow.com/story/18894210/kasich-signs-human-trafficking-bill-in-toledo

[23]. July 20, 2011. Joe Guillen, "Gov. John Kasich signs late-term abortion ban into law," *Cleveland Plain Dealer*, July 20, 2011:

http://www.cleveland.com/open/index.ssf/2011/07/gov_kasich_signs_late-term_abo.html

[24]. 2012 State of the State Address, Steubenville, Ohio, February 6, 2012. Reginald Fields, "Ohio Gov. John Kasich declares 'Ohio is alive again' in his second State of the State speech," Cleveland *Plain Dealer*, February 7, 2012: http://www.cleveland.com/open/index.ssf/2012/02/ohio_gov_john_kasich_declares.html

[25] Twitter post, July 26, 2011. http://twitter.com/#!/johnkasich

[26]. Interview in Columbus, March 29, 2012. Mark Niquette, "Dogma Crumbles as Kasich Fights Own Party to Tax Ohio's Drillers," *Bloomberg.com*, April 3, 2012: http://webfarm.bloomberg.com/news/2012-04-03/dogma-crumbles-as-kasich-fights-own-party-to-tax-ohio-s-drillers.html

[27]. Speech to a lobbyist luncheon at Brio Tuscan Grille at Polaris, Columbus, OH, November 4, 2010. Jim Siegel and Mark Niquette, "Kasich lays down law to lobbyists," *Columbus Dispatch*, November 5, 2010: http://www.dispatch.com/content/stories/local/2010/11/05/kasich-lays-down-the-law.html

[28]. Interview with Jo Ingles. Jo Ingles, "Gov. Kasich praises recent accomplishments of Ohio's legislature," WKSU-FM, June 14, 2012: http://www.wksu.org/news/story/32040

[29]. Speaking at a college in Columbus, Ohio, November 28, 2011. David Taintor, "Kasich: 'My Life Is A Lot Better' Without Newspapers," *Talking Points Memo*, November 29, 2011: http://tpmdc.talkingpointsmemo.com/2011/11/kasich-my-life-is-a-lot-better-without-newspapers.php?ref=fpnewsfeed

[30]. Joe Vardon and Jim Siegel, "Issue 2 foes lack identity," *Columbus Dispatch*, November 3, 2011: http://www.dispatch.com/content/stories/local/2011/11/03/issue-2-foes-lack-identity.html

[31]. October 31, 2011, Zanesville, Ohio. PolitiFact Ohio, "John Kasich slams use of out-of-state arbitrators in contract talks with safety forces," *PolitiFact Ohio*, November 3, 2011: http://www.politifact.com/ohio/statements/2011/nov/03/john-kasich/john-kasich-slams-use-out-state-arbitrators-contra/

[32]. Interview with Alan Colmes on Colmes' Fox News Radio talk show, June 17, 2010. Reginald Fields, "John Kasich not joining the chorus begging LeBron James to stay," Cleveland *Plain Dealer*, June 21, 2010: http://www.cleveland.com/open/index.ssf/2010/06/ohio_governor_candidate_not_jo.html

[33]. Remarks to the 32d Annual Holocaust Commemoration at the Ohio Statehouse, Columbus, April 17, 2012. Jo Inglis, "Kasich says Holocaust Memorial is coming to the Statehouse," WKSU-FM Radio, April 17, 2012: http://www.wksu.org/news/story/31395

[34]. Jim Provance, "Kasich says rules prevent hiring Ohio's best," *Toledo Blade*, December 17, 2010: http://print.toledoblade.com/State/2010/12/17/Kasich-says-rules-prevent-hiring-Ohio-s-best.html

[35]. Interview with David Gregory on NBC-TV's "Meet The Press," April 15, 2012. Henry J. Gomez, "Gov. John Kasich's economic optimism could lift

President Barack Obama in Ohio: Analysis," Cleveland *Plain Dealer*, April 17, 2012:
http://www.cleveland.com/open/index.ssf/2012/04/gov_john_kasichs_economic_opti.html

[36]. 2012 State of the State Address, Steubenville, Ohio, February 7, 2012. Reginald Fields, "Ohio Gov. John Kasich declares Ohio is 'alive again' in his second State of the State speech," Cleveland *Plain Dealer*, February 7, 2012:
http://www.cleveland.com/open/index.ssf/2012/02/ohio_gov_john_kasich_declares.html

[37]. March, 2011. Reginald Fields, "Ohio Gov. John Kasich counts on liquor consumption to bring jobs," Cleveland *Plain Dealer*, March 22, 2011:
jobshttp://www.cleveland.com/open/index.ssf/2011/03/ohio_gov_john_kasich_hopes_boo.html

[38]. October 2011. Darrel Rowland, "Poll: Issue 2 sinking", *Columbus Dispatch*, October 26, 2011:
http://www.dispatch.com/content/stories/local/2011/10/26/poll-issue-2-sinking.html

[39]. Joe Vardon, "Fun and politics mix as Kasich opens fair," *Columbus Dispatch*, July 28, 2011.
http://www.dispatch.com/content/stories/general/2011/07/28/fun-and-politics-mix-as-kasich-opens-fair.html

Paul LePage:

[1]. Rebekah Metzler, "LePage fields questions on budget in Newcastle," *Portland Press Herald*, May 21, 2011: http://www.pressherald.com/news/lepage-fields-questions-on-budget-in-newcastle_2011-05-21.html

[2]. Susan Sharon, "LePage's temperament becomes campaign issue, Maine Public Broadcasting Network, September 29, 2010:
http://www.mpbn.net/Home/tabid/36/ctl/ViewItem/mid/3478/ItemId/13704/Default.aspx

[3]. Jessica Taylor, "LePage: I'd tell Obama to 'go to hell,'" *Politico*, September 29, 2010: http://www.politico.com/news/stories/0910/42886.html

[4]. Kevin Miller, "LePage dismisses BPA dangers; 'worst case is some women may have little beards,'" *Bangor Daily News*, February 23, 2011:
http://bangordailynews.com/2011/02/22/politics/gov-lepage-dismisses-dangers-of-bpa/

[5]. Susan Cover, "UPDATE: LePage tells NAACP to "kiss my butt," *Portland Press Herald*, January 14, 2011: http://www.pressherald.com/news/LePage-tells-NAACP-to-kiss-my-butt.html

[6]. Laura Clawson, **"**Looking to Weaken Child Labor Laws, GOPer Says Working at 11 Years Old "Not a Big Deal," "Doesn't Hurt Anybody," *AlterNet*, April 2011:
http://www.alternet.org/rss/1/571882/looking_to_weaken_child_labor_laws,_goper_says_working_at_11_years_old_%5C%22not_a_big_deal,%5C%22_%5C%22doesn%5C%27t_hurt_anybody%5C%22/

[7]. "LePage brings 'Capitol' to Sagadahoc County," *Times Record*, April 22, 2011:
http://www.timesrecord.com/articles/2011/04/26/news/doc4db59fdb85e0f046941001.txt

[8]. Mark LaFlamme, "LePage wows Franco crowd in Lewiston," *Sun Journal*, March 17, 2011: http://www.sunjournal.com/LePage0317

[9]. Gerald Weinand, "LePage Steps in it, Wrong on bull semen," *Dirigo Blue*, October 6, 2010: http://dirigoblue.com.lb.soapblox.net/diary/1998/lepage-steps-in-it-wrong-on-bull-semen

[10]. Susan Cover. "LePage faces feisty Rockport town hall. *Morning Sentinel*, June 18, 2011: http://www.onlinesentinel.com/news/lepage-faces-fiesty-rockport-town-hall_2011-06-17.html?pageType=mobile&id=1

[11]. Susan Sharon, "LePage: Environmental Groups Have Too Much Power," Maine Public Broadcasting, August 24, 2010: http://www.mpbn.net/Home/tabid/36/ctl/ViewItem/mid/3478/ItemId/13295/Default.aspx

[12]. Susan Cover, "LePage faces feisty Rockport town hall," *Morning Sentinel*, June 18, 2011: http://www.onlinesentinel.com/news/lepage-faces-fiesty-rockport-town-hall_2011-06-17.html?pageType=mobile&id=1

[13]. "LePage Snubs National Governor's Association Meeting," Maine Public Broadcasting Network, July 15, 2011: http://www.mpbn.net/Home/tabid/36/ctl/ViewItem/mid/3478/ItemId/17235/Default.aspx

[14]. Susan Cover, "GOP forum: Sunday hunting splits candidates," *Kennebec Journal*, March 12, 2010: http://www.kjonline.com/news/sunday-hunting-splits-candidates.html

[15]. Christopher Cousins, "LePage says Maine students looked down upon, unveils a new education initiatives," *Bangor Daily News*, July 25, 2012: http://bangordailynews.com/2012/07/25/politics/lepage-blasts-education-system-unveils-new-initiatives/

[16]. Susan Cover, "Winter heat aid expected to drop," *Kennebec Journal*, July 25, 2011: http://www.kjonline.com/news/winter-heat-aid-expected-to-drop_2011-07-24.html

[17]. Michael Shepherd, "Rally rails against 'toxic' teacher dialogue," *The Maine Campus*, March 27, 2011: http://mainecampus.com/2011/03/27/umf-education-students-rally-against-toxic-teacher-dialogue/

[18]. Bill Trotter, "At Fishermen's Forum, LePage calls for more processing, fewer regulations," Bangor Daily News, March 4, 2011: http://bangordailynews.com/2011/03/04/business/at-fishermen%E2%80%99s-forum-lepage-calls-for-more-processing-fewer-regulations/

[19]. Carolyn Callahan, "Governor Paul LePage Shares Personal Story of Homelessness", WABI-TV (Bangor), February 24, 2011: http://www.wabi.tv/news/18174/governor-paul-lepage-shares-personal-story-of-homelessness

[20]. Associated Press, "LePage receives honorary degree from Husson," *Portland Press Herald*, May 14, 2011: http://www.pressherald.com/news/LePage-to-receive-honorary-degree-from-Husson-.html

[21]. Steven Bertoni, "Ready for Business," *Forbes*, December 30, 2010: http://www.forbes.com/forbes/2011/0117/focus-paul-lepage-maine-republican-ready-for-business.html

[22]. Governor LePage's Weekly Radio Address: There's No Excuse for Domestic

Violence, July 9, 2011:
http://www.maine.gov/tools/whatsnew/index.php?topic=Gov_Radio_Addresses&id=266895&v=article

[23]. Susan Calder, "LePage pitches in for homeless," Waterville *Morning Sentinel*, May 24, 2011: http://www.onlinesentinel.com/news/lepage-pitches-in-for-homeless_2011-05-23.html

[24]. Chris Rose, "Governor LePage recalls difficult childhood," WCSH-TV (Portland), July 6, 2011:
http://www.wcsh6.com/news/article/164847/2/Governor-LePage-recalls-difficult-childhood

[25]. WMTW-TV, "Caught on Tape: Gov. LePage Snaps at Media," July 28, 2011:
http://www.wmtw.com/news/28697661/detail.html#ixzz1TTIsoKKa

[26]. Eric Russell, "LePage says political antics in Washington have cost Americans", *Bangor Daily News,* August 6, 2011:
http://bangordailynews.com/2011/08/06/politics/lepage-says-political-antics-in-washington-has-cost-americans/

[27]. Judy Harrison, "Mainers pray for nation at LePage's request, *Bangor Daily News*, August 6, 2011:
http://bangordailynews.com/2011/08/06/news/bangor/group-prays-for-nation-at-cascade-park-event/

[28]. Eric Russell, "During Bangor refueling wing visit, Le Page calls cuts 'until it hurts'". *Bangor Daily News,* August 9, 2011:
http://bangordailynews.com/2011/08/09/politics/during-bangor-refueling-wing-visit-lepage-calls-for-cuts-%E2%80%98until-it-hurts%E2%80%99/?ref=mostReadBox

[29]. Andi Parkinson, "LePage Calls Saturday Unemployed Constituent Meeting "Bull Shit"; Stresses Disdain," *Dirigo Blue*, December 4, 2011:
http://www.dirigoblue.com/2011/12/05/gov-lepage-calls-saturday-unemployed-constituent-meeting-bull-shit-stresses-disdain/#comment-87

[30]. A. J. Higgins, "Governor LePage Attends MLK Breakfast in Waterville," MPBN, January 16, 2012:
http://www.mpbn.net/News/MaineNewsArchive/tabid/181/ctl/ViewItem/mid/3475/ItemId/19811/Default.aspx

[31]. Colin Woodard, "Maine: LePage on "Tea Party" staffer," *World Wide Woodard* blog, July 24, 2010: http://colinwoodard.blogspot.com/2010/07/maine-lepage-on-tea-party-staffer.html

[32]. Eric Russell, "LePage softens tone in Bangor visit,", *Bangor Daily News*, October 5, 2010: http://bangordailynews.com/2010/10/05/politics/lepage-softens-tone-in-bangor-visit/

[33]. John Richardson, "LePage's first year: 'contentious', 'extreme', and, yes, 'effective,'" *Portland Press Herald*, January 8, 2012:
http://www.pressherald.com/news/extreme_2012-01-08.html

[34]. Julie Daigle, "UPDATED-Governor says to Paradis, 'I don't know what planet you're on" (with video). *Fiddlehead Focus*, December 27, 2011:
http://www.fiddleheadfocus.com/story/updated-governor-says-paradis-i-dont-know-what-planet-youre-video5765

[35]. Ann S. Kim, "State workers 'corrupted by bureaucracy," Portland Press

Herald, April 28, 2012: http://www.pressherald.com/news/LePage-responds-to-critics-after-calling-state-workers-corrupt.html

[36]. Letter from Governor LePage to State Employees, April 27, 2012: http://unmasker4maine.files.wordpress.com/2012/04/gov-lepage-letter-to-state-employees.pdf

[37]. Interview with Phil Harriman on the "Inside Maine with Phil Harriman Show" on WGAN Radio, Portland, March 31, 2012: http://www.wgan.com/Inside-Maine/2763516

[38]. Speaking in New York City at the Bush Institute Conference on Taxes and Economic Growth, April 10, 2012. Mal Leary, "LePage tells New York City audience about his goals to reduce Maine taxes," Bangor Daily News, April 11, 2012: http://bangordailynews.com/2012/04/10/politics/lepage-tells-new-york-city-audience-about-his-goals-to-reduce-maine-taxes/?utm_source=BDN+News+Updates&utm_campaign=8d3d890576-RSS_MORNINGUPDATE_EMAIL_CAMPAIGN&utm_medium=email

[39]. Susan Cover, "TABOR III in works," Waterville Morning Sentinel, April 16, 2012: http://www.onlinesentinel.com/news/tabor-iii-in-works_2012-04-15.html

[40]. Christian Civic League of Maine, "Governor joins over 500 in rally to save unborn Mainers," January 14, 2012: http://www.cclmaine.org/governor-joins-over-500-in-rally-to-save-unborn-mainers/

[41]. Glenn Adams (AP), "Paul LePage Sworn In as Governor," Portland Press Herald, January 6, 2011: http://www.pressherald.com/news/maine-Paul-LePage-sworn-in-as-Maine-governor.html

[42]. Kevin Miller, "Lawmakers weigh in on LePage's first 100 days," Bangor Daily News, April 13, 2011: http://bangordailynews.com/2011/04/13/politics/lawmakers-weigh-in-on-lepage%E2%80%99s-first-100-days/

[43]. Steve Mistler, "'We have nothing to do': LePage slams Legislature for lack of progress," Sun-Journal, April 14, 2011: http://www.sunjournal.com/state/story/1015225

[44]. Susan Sharon, "Mural Comes Down at Governor's Request But Dispute Continues, Maine Public Broadcasting Network, March 28, 2011: http://www.mpbn.net/home/tabid/36/ctl/viewitem/mid/3478/itemid/15776/default.aspx

[45] Caroline Cornish, "Governor LePage stands by his mural decision," WCSH (Portland), March 25, 2011: http://www.wcsh6.com/news/article/153122/314/Governor-LePage-stands-by-h

[46]. "LePage: GOP Meeting About 'Zipping My Mouth," Maine Public Broadcasting, March 31, 2011: http://www.mpbn.net/Home/tabid/36/ctl/ViewItem/mid/3478/ItemId/15824/Default.aspx

[47]. Letter from Paul LePage to Rep. Pingree of Maine's First Congressional District, regarding her letter opposing LePage's attempt to reduce Medicaid eligibility, July 11, 2012. Posted at Dirigo Blue (blog): http://bangordailynews.com/link/dirigo-blue/A

[48]. Eric Russell, "'Get off the couch and get yourself a job': LePage talks welfare reform at GOP convention," Bangor Daily News, May 6, 2012:

http://bangordailynews.com/2012/05/06/politics/get-off-the-couch-and-get-yourself-a-job-lepage-talks-welfare-reform-at-gop-convention/

[49]. Christopher Cousins, "LePage urges Thomas College graduates to seize their own destinies," Bangor Daily News, May 13, 2012:
http://bangordailynews.com/2012/05/12/news/mid-maine/lepage-urges-thomas-college-graduates-to-seize-their-own-destinies/?utm_source=BDN+News+Updates&utm_campaign=55291e39a9-RSS_MORNINGUPDATE_EMAIL_CAMPAIGN&utm_medium=email

[50]. Alex Barber, "Domestic violence, 'a very serious problem,' LePage tells students at Penobscot Jobs Corps," *Bangor Daily News*, June 22, 2012:
"http://bangordailynews.com/2012/06/22/politics/lepage-visits-penobscot-job-corps-calls-domestic-violence-a-very-serious-problem/

[51]. Radio Address: Growing the Maine Economy, June 25, 2012:
http://www.maine.gov/tools/whatsnew/index.php?topic=Gov_Radio_Addresses&id=399648&v=article

[52]. Governor Paul LePage Releases Statement Regarding US Supreme Court's Ruling on the PPACA," June 28, 2012:
http://www.maine.gov/tools/whatsnew/index.php?topic=Portal+News&id=403449&v=article-2011

[53]. Radio Address: Obamacare is on Hold in Maine, July 7, 2012:
http://www.maine.gov/tools/whatsnew/index.php?topic=Gov_Radio_Addresses&id=409717&v=article

[54]. Statement of Governor LePage on Gestapo Comment, July 9, 2012:
http://www.maine.gov/tools/whatsnew/index.php?topic=Gov+News&id=409920&v=article2011

[55]. "LePage questioned about 'Gestapo' remark," WMTW.com, (Author's transcription of video), July 9, 2012:
http://www.wmtw.com/news/maine/LePage-questioned-about-Gestapo-remark/-/8792012/15452054/-/s261ktz/-/index.html

[56]. Paul Heintz, "At Brock Fundraiser, Maine Gov. Paul LePage Doubles Down on "Gestapo" Comment," *Seven Days*, July 12, 2012:
http://7d.blogs.com/blurt/2012/07/maine-gov-paul-lepage-doubles-down-on-gestapo-comment-after-brock-fundraiser.html

[57]. "LePage and reporter spar over IRS comments," YouTube, uploaded July 12, 2012.
http://www.youtube.com/watch?v=6BCm9QtYOGQ&feature=player_embedded#!

[58]. Radio Address, July 13, 2012:
http://www.maine.gov/tools/whatsnew/index.php?topic=Gov_Radio_Addresses&id=410064&v=article

Susana Martinez:
[1]. Source: Campaign website, susanamartinez2010.com, "On the Issues," November 2, 2010, as posted by On The Issues.org:
http://www.ontheissues.org/Governor/Susana_Martinez_Crime.htm

[2. Darren Samuelsohn, "GOP candidates know global warming," *Politico*, August 18, 2010: http://dyn.politico.com/printstory.cfm?uuid=82C45B00-18FE-70B2-

[3]. Jennifer Rubin, "Interview with Susana Martinez," *Washington Post* "Right Turn" blog, January 24, 2011:
http://voices.washingtonpost.com/right-turn/2011/01/interview_gov_susana_martinez.html

[4]. Fox News Latino /Associated Press, "Susana Martínez Tells Police to Check Immigration Status in New Mexico," Fox News Latino, February 1, 2011:
http://latino.foxnews.com/latino/politics/2011/02/01/new-mexico-governor-susana-martinez-tells-police-check-immigration-status/#ixzz1SCVG49mD

[5]. Michael Haederle, "A rising GOP star in Santa Fe," *Los Angeles Times,* January 1, 2011: http://articles.latimes.com/2011/jan/01/nation/la-na-susana-martinez-20110101/2

[6]. Elliot Spagat, Associated Press, "US-Mexico governors' conference languishes," CNSNews.com, September 29, 2011:
http://cnsnews.com/news/article/us-mexico-governors-conference-languishes

[7]. Interview with KLUZ-TV, Univision's Albuquerque affiliate, as reported by the Associated Press. *International Business Times* Staff Reporter, "New Mexico Governor Susana Martinez Admits Grandparents Came to U.S. Illegally, People Take to Twitter," *International Business Times,* September 8, 2011:
http://www.ibtimes.com/articles/210904/20110908/new-mexico-governor-susana-martinez-grandparents-illegal-immigrants-twitter.htm

[8]. Samantha Manning, "Governor Defends Packed Agenda, Pushes for Repealing Immigration Law," KFOX-TV (El Paso, Texas Fox Affiliate), October 24, 2011:
http://www.kfoxtv.com/news/29121672/detail.html

[9]. Interview with KOAT-TV (ABC affiliate, Albuquerque) at the 40th Albuquerque International Balloon Fiesta, October 9, 2011:
http://www.koat.com/balloon-fiesta-extended-coverage/29432468/detail.html#ixzz1bjK8LfmG

[10]. Interview with *New Mexico in Focus* during the 2010 gubernatorial campaign. Steven Ertelt, "Pro-Life Gov. Susana Martinez 'Humbled' by Vice-President Talk," LifeNews.com, August 30, 2011:
http://www.lifenews.com/2011/08/30/pro-life-gov-susana-martinez-humbled-by-vice-president-talk/

[11]. News conference statement. Milan Simonich (Texas-New Mexico Newspapers), "Gov. Martinez: New DNA law imprisoning more killers and rapists," *Carlsbad Current-Argus,* July 6, 2012:
http://www.currentargus.com/carlsbad-news/ci_21023770/gov-martinez-new-dna-law-imprisoning-more-killers?source=rss

[12.] Statement issued after the 2012 Supreme Court ruling concerning Arizona and immigration. Milan Simonich, "Groups support Supreme Court ruling that results in Ariz. immigration law strike downs," Farmington, NM *Daily Times*, June 25, 2012: http://www.daily-times.com/farmington-news/ci_20937818/groups-support-supreme-court-ruling-that-results-ariz?source=rss

[13]. Andrew Romano, "Susana Martinez: What New Mexico's Governor Can Teach the GOP," *Newsweek*, May 14, 2012:
http://www.thedailybeast.com/newsweek/2012/05/13/susana-martinez-what-new-mexico-s-governor-can-teach-the-gop.html

[14]. Statement issued by Martinez after a federal indictment of members of an alleged illegal driver's license distribution ring. Associated Press, "5 New Mexico residents linked to immigrant driver's license fraud ring," *FoxNews.com*, June 20, 2012: http://www.foxnews.com/us/2012/06/20/5-new-mexico-residents-linked-to-immigrant-driver-license-fraud-ring/

[15]. Jeri Clausing (AP), "Noble animals, ignoble fates", *Philly.com*, June 10, 2012: http://articles.philly.com/2012-06-10/news/32157041_1_horse-slaughter-industry-horse-slaughter-horse-industry

[16]. Interview with KOAT-TV reporter Tanya Mendiz, "Loophole lets online predators skip registration," KOAT-TV (Albuquerque ABC affiliate), February 19, 2012: http://www.koat.com/Loophole-Lets-Online-Predators-Skip-Registration/-/9154444/9714056/-/18i737/-/index.html

[17]. Sandra Baltazar Martinez, "Faces of Immigration: Martinez, granddaughter of immigrants, rules with her head, not her heart," Santa Fe *New Mexican*, July 31, 2011: http://www.santafenewmexican.com/localnews/FACES-OF-IMMIGRATION-Ruling-with-her-head-not-heart-Ever-a-pro

Butch Otter

[1]. David Weigel, "Butch Otter rides again," *Reason*, November 2006: http://reason.com/archives/2006/10/31/butch-otter-rides-again/singlepage

[2]. Associated Press, 'Gov. Otter vetoes bill to block Obamacare," *Idaho Press-Tribune*, April 20, 2011:
 http://www.idahopress.com/news/state/article_cfedb424-6b7b-11e0-93ce-001cc4c002e0.html

[3]. Erika Bolstad, "Potatoes promote weight gain? Spud slander, Idaho says," *The Kansas City Star*, July 24, 2011:
http://www.kansascity.com/2011/07/24/3033365/potatoes-promote-weight-gain-spud.html#storylink=rss#ixzz1To2OvIKj

[4]. Joel Connelly, "Connelly: Has twilight come for America's wolves,?" *Seattle Post-Intelligencer*, June 5, 2011:
http://www.seattlepi.com/local/connelly/article/Has-Twilight-Come-for-America-s-Wolves-Lets-1408974.php

[5]. Dustin Hurst, "Idaho solons deride wolf de-listing, say the state can manage its own affairs," *IdahoReporter.com*, August 6, 2010:
http://www.idahoreporter.com/2010/idaho-solons-deride-wolf-de-listing-say-the-state-can-manage-its-own-affairs/

[6]. Nathaniel Hoffnam, "Cope Keeps Butch Up at Night," *Boise Weekly*, February 24, 2010: http://www.boiseweekly.com/CityDesk/archives/2010/02/24/cope-keeps-butch-up-at-night

[7]. Spokane *Spokesman-Review*, March 14, 2007, p. B1:
 http://www.library.umaine.edu/auth/EZProxy/test/authej.asp?url=http://search.proquest.com.prxy8.ursus.maine.edu/docview/395038551?accountid=27252

[8]. Betsy Z. Russell, "Otter off to fast start," Spokane *Spokesman-Review*, February 13, 2007: http://www.spokesmanreview.com/tools/story_pf.asp?ID=174103

[9]. Betsy Z. Russell, "Otter blasts ID bill he co-sponsored," *Spokane Spokesman-Review*, February 23, 2007:
http://www.spokesman.com/stories/2007/feb/23/otter-blasts-id-bill-he-co-

sponsored/

[10]. Betsy Z. Russell, "Otter's City Club Visit a Pleasant One," Spokane *Spokesman-Review*, February 25, 2007:
http://www.spokesman.com/stories/2007/feb/25/otters-city-club-visit-a-pleasant-one/

[11]. Jessie L. Bonner (AP), "Governor Otter Enlists Democrats in Fight to Enact New Idaho Education Laws," MagicValley.com, February 1, 2012:
http://magicvalley.com/news/state-and-regional/governor-otter-enlists-democrats-help-in-fight-to-enact/article_d1e5fb5e-4cdc-11e1-8b16-001871e3ce6c.html#ixzz1sEUbHVNe

[12]. D.F. Olveira, "Quotable Quote: Gov. Butch Otter," Spokane *Spokesman-Review*, February 2, 2012:
http://www.spokesman.com/blogs/hbo/2012/feb/02/quotable-quote-gov-butch-otter/

[13]. Interview with Neil Cavuto on "Your World with Neil Cavuto," Fox News Channel, March 18, 2012:
http://www.foxnews.com/story/0,2933,589662,00.html#ixzz1sEY6JcVZ

[14]. David Cole, "Butch stumps for Mitt," CDAPress.com, March 6, 2012:
http://www.cdapress.com/news/political/article_4b0d32f1-f2e5-5b47-9f5a-f49618404562.html

[15]. Laura Zuckerman, "Idaho governor signs abortion ban after 20 weeks," Reuters, April 14, 2012: http://www.reuters.com/article/2011/04/14/us-abortion-idaho-idUSTRE73D7AB20110414

[16]. Paul Foy, "Nuclear engineers gather for Utah conference," Ogden *Standard-Examiner* (AP), May 14, 2012:
http://www.standard.net/stories/2012/05/14/nuclear-engineers-gather-utah-conference

[17]. News Release, "Governor Signs Idaho Health Freedom Act," March 17, 2010.
http://gov.idaho.gov/mediacenter/press/pr2010/prmar10/pr_023.html

Sean Parnell:

[1]. Column by Sean Parnell, "Habitat designation won't help polar bears, but will kill Alaska's jobs," *Washington Post,* August 6, 2010:
http://www.washingtonpost.com/wp-dyn/content/article/2010/08/05/AR2010080505136.html

[2]. Sean Cockerham, "Parnell slices $400 million from Legislature's capital spending," *Anchorage Daily News*, June 30, 2011:
http://www.thenewstribune.com/2011/06/29/v-printerfriendly/1726190/parnell-budget-vetoes-top-400.html#ixzz1Rp87x2xS

[3]. Associated Press, "Debt deal likely to put hurt on states, poor," CBS News, July 31, 2011:
http://www.cbsnews.com/stories/2011/07/31/politics/main20086124.shtml?tag=cbsContentWrap;cbsContent

[4]. Nick Wing, "Sean Parnell: 'Only God Knows' How Old Earth Is," *Huffington Post*, October 29, 2010: http://www.huffingtonpost.com/2010/10/29/sean-parnell-age-of-the-earth_n_776215.html

[5]. Sean Parnell, "Federal wetlands guidelines are land grab," *Anchorage Daily News*,

August 9, 2011: http://www.adn.com/2011/08/07/2004511/federal-wetlands-guidelines-are.html

[6] Pat Forgey, "Parnell pushes for Senate approval of tax bill," *The Juneau Empire*, April 5, 2011: http://juneauempire.com/local/2011-04-05/parnell-pushes-senate-approval-oil-tax-bill

[7]. Letter to the 12th Annual Interdenominational Prayer Service for the Unborn, January 21, 2012: http://www.catholicanchor.org/wordpress/wp-content/uploads/2012/01/Gov-Parnells-Ltr-to-ProLife-Gp-2012.pdf

[8]. Pat Forgey, "Questions about sex trafficking bill remain," *The Juneau Empire*, June 21, 2012: http://juneauempire.com/local/2012-06-21/questions-about-sex-trafficking-bill-remain

[9]. Russell Stigall, "Parnell: Tax reform must include existing fields," *The Juneau Empire*, April 20, 2012: http://juneauempire.com/local/2012-04-20/parnell-tax-reform-must-include-existing-fields

[10]. Pat Forgey, "Parnell blasts Senate education 'giveaway,'" *The Juneau Empire*, February 15, 2012: http://juneauempire.com/state/2012-02-15

[11]. Becky Bohrer (AP), "Parnell wants Alaska divested from companies in business with Iran," *The Juneau Empire*, February 2, 2012: http://juneauempire.com/state/2012-02-02/parnell-wants-alaska-divested-companies-business-iran

[12]. Pat Forgey, "Governor acts to create Native language council," *The Juneau Empire*, May 31, 2012: http://juneauempire.com/local/2012-05-31/governor-acts-create-native-language-council

[13]. Emily Miller, "Alaska's regulation stranglehold," *The Washington Times*, August 30, 2011: http://www.washingtontimes.com/blog/watercooler/2011/aug/30/miller-alaskas-regulation-stranglehold/

[14] Becky Bohrer (AP), "Parnell warns 'disaster' awaits if changes aren't made," *The Juneau Empire*, July 21, 2011: http://juneauempire.com/state/2011-07-21/parnell-warns-disaster-awaits-if-changes-arent-made

[15]. State of the State Address, January 20, 2010: http://gov.alaska.gov/parnell/press-room/full-press-release.html?pr=5246

[16]. Speech: Alaska's Rare Opportunity, September 30, 2011: http://gov.alaska.gov/parnell/press-room/full-press-release.html?pr=5917

[17]. Speech to the National Press Club on "America's Energy Security," February 25, 2011: http://gov.alaska.gov/parnell/press-room/full-press-release.html?pr=5665

[18]. 2011 State of the State address, January 19, 2011: http://gov.alaska.gov/parnell/press-room/full-press-release.html?pr=5626

[19] Speech to the National Association of Attorney Generals, June 19, 2012: http://gov.alaska.gov/parnell/press-room/full-press-release.html?pr=6180

[20] Speech, Rural Providers Conference, May 28, 2012: http://gov.alaska.gov/parnell/press-room/full-press-release.html?pr=6154

[21]. Speech, Blessing of the Fleet, May 5, 2012: http://gov.alaska.gov/parnell/press-room/full-press-release.html?pr=6124

[22]. State of the State speech, January 19, 2012: http://gov.alaska.gov/parnell/press-room/full-press-release.html?pr=6011

[23]. Remarks on the Supreme Court decision on the Affordable Care Act, June 28, 2012: http://gov.alaska.gov/parnell/press-room/full-press-release.html?pr=6185

Rick Perry

[1]. Speaking on the Laura Ingraham radio show. JoAnne Allen (Reuters), "Republican Perry labels Washington a 'seedy place," Reuters, August 25, 2011: http://www.reuters.com/article/2011/08/26/usa-campaign-perry-seedy-idUSN1E77O1YR20110826

[2]. R. G. Ratcliffe, "Perry says Texas can leave the Union it wants to," *Houston Chronicle* Texas Politics blog: http://blogs.chron.com/texaspolitics/archives/2009/04/perry_says_texa.html

[3] Press Release, "Gov. Perry Issues Proclamation for Days of Prayer for Rain in Texas," April 21, 2011: http://governor.state.tx.us/news/proclamation/16038/

[4]. Steve Benen, "Perry sees Biblical purpose for economic troubles," *Washington Monthly*'s Political Animal blog, June 13, 2011: http://www.washingtonmonthly.com/political-animal/2011_06/perry_sees_biblical_purpose_fo030231.php

[5]. State of the State address, February 8, 2011: http://governor.state.tx.us/news/speech/15673/

[6]. Andy Barr, "Texas-sized gaffe: Rick Perry says Juarez is 'in America,'" *Politico*, March 1, 2012: http://www.politico.com/news/stories/0211/50368.html#ixzz1Rp45ZTbq

[7]. Jake Sherman, "Rick Perry: Oil spill may be 'act of God,'" May 3, 2010: http://www.politico.com/news/stories/0510/36691.html

[8]. Andy Barr, "Rick Perry: Tea Party darling," *Politico*, April 15, 2009 : http://www.politico.com/news/stories/0409/21295.html

[9]. "Gov. Rick Perry says the federal government regulates how much salt we can put on our food: False," PolitiFact Texas, November, 2, 2010: http://www.politifact.com/texas/statements/2010/nov/06/rick-perry/gov-rick-perry-says-federal-government-regulates-h/

[10]. NBC News-Facebook debate, January 8, 2012: http://presspass.msnbc.msn.com/_news/2012/01/08/10049650-read-the-nbc-news-facebook-debate-transcript

[11]. Editorial, "The Tea Party Cowboy," *The Register-Guard* (Eugene, Oregon), November 17, 2010, p. A10: http://special.registerguard.com/csp/cms/sites/web/opinion/25550361-47/perry-cowboy-kitzhaber-texas-kinds.csp

[12]. Michael Falcone, "Rick Perry Accuses Obama Of Leaving Astronauts To 'Hitchhike Into Space,'" ABC News, July 21, 2011: http://blogs.abcnews.com/thenote/2011/07/rick-perry-accuses-obama-of-leaving-astronauts-to-hitchhike-into-space.html

[13]. Speech at Longview, Texas, May 23, 2011. *Snopes.com*, "Rick Perry Speech" (certified as "correctly attributed" by Snopes), July 11, 2011: http://www.snopes.com/politics/soapbox/rickperry.asp

[14]. From Perry's appearance at "The Response", a prayer event at Reliant Stadium in Houston: Joe Holley, "Perry offers praise, prayer but little on politics,"*Houston Chronicle,* August 7, 2011:
 http://www.chron.com/disp/story.mpl/metropolitan/7686497.html#ixzz1UNL4onv4

[15]. From Perry's appearance at "The Response," a prayer event at Reliant Stadium in Houston: David Magee, "Ready or Not, America, Here Comes Rick Perry: Presidential Candidate," *International Business Times*, August 7, 2011: http://www.ibtimes.com/articles/193825/20110807/rick-perry-presidential-candidate-republican-race.htm

[16]. Announcing "The Response," a prayer event at Reliant Stadium in Houston: Sean Wardwell, "Carnival of Faith," *McPherson Sentinel* (KS) , June 8, 2011:
http://www.mcphersonsentinel.com/opinions/columnists/x795261741/Carnival-of-faith

[17]. Matt Loffman and Mark Murray, "Jose Cuevas, you are a friend of mine," *NBC News First Read*, June 24, 2011:
http://firstread.msnbc.msn.com/_news/2011/06/24/6934735-jose-cuevas-you-are-a-friend-of-mine

[18]. Arlette Saenz, "Rick Perry Hits Bernanke and Fed," *The Note* blog, *ABC News*, September 29, 2011:
http://abcnews.go.com/blogs/politics/2011/09/rick-perry-hits-bernanke-and-fed-talks-immigration-and-border-security/

[19]. Interview with CNBC, September 29, 2011. Arlette Saenz, "Rick Perry Hits Bernanke and Fed," *The Note* blog, *ABC News*, September 29, 2011:
http://abcnews.go.com/blogs/politics/2011/09/rick-perry-hits-bernanke-and-fed-talks-immigration-and-border-security/

[20]. W. Gardner Selby and Asher Price, "Perry's strong views on climate change can be muted at home," *Austin American-Statesman*, October 21, 2007:
http://www.statesman.com/news/content/region/legislature/stories/10/21/1021govwarming.html

[21]. Evan McMorris-Santoro, "Rick Perry: Climate Change Is A Hoax Drummed Up By Scientists Looking To Make Money," *Talking Points Memo*, August 17, 2011.: http://tpmdc.talkingpointsmemo.com/2011/08/rick-perry-climate-change-is-a-hoax-drummed-up-by-scientists-looking-to-make-money.php?ref=fpa

[22]. "Rick Perry says federal bureaucrats will take over local building codes," PolitiFact, October 28, 2011: http://www.politifact.com/truth-o-meter/statements/2011/nov/15/rick-perry/rick-perry-says-federal-bureaucrats-will-take-over/

[23]. Lara Seligman, "Rick Perry Would Say No to VP Slot", *National Journal*, March 22, 2012: http://nationaljournal.com/2012-presidential-campaign/rick-perry-would-say-no-to-vp-slot-20120322

[24]. Interview with CNBC's John Harwood. Zeke Miller, "Rick Perry is Really Doubling Down on the Birther Stuff," *Business Insider*, October 25, 2011:
http://articles.businessinsider.com/2011-10-25/politics/30319132_1_birther-issue-interview-texas-gov#ixzz1sDu89TZx

[25]. Mark Benjamin, "Perry Compared Homosexuality to Alcoholism in 2008 Book," *Time* Magazine Swampland Political Blog, August 24, 2011: http://swampland.time.com/2011/08/24/perry-compared-homosexuality-to-alcoholism-in-2008-book/

[26] Speaking in Iowa at a radio forum organized by pro-life group Personhood USA, December 2011. Catalina Camia, "Rick Perry has 'transformation' of his abortion views," *USA Today* On Politics Blog, December 27, 2011: http://content.usatoday.com/communities/onpolitics/post/2011/12/rick-perry-abortion-gift-of-life-/1

[27]. Leigh Frillici, "Governor Perry's Prayer Event at Reliant Stadium Draws Criticism," KHOU-TV (Houston CBS affiliate), July 24, 2011: http://www.khou.com/news/local/Governor-Perrys-prayer-event-at-Reliant-Stadium-draws-criticism-126093278.html

[28]. Press Release, "Gov Perry Declares August 6th a Day of Prayer," June 6, 2011: http://governor.state.tx.us/news/proclamation/16247/

[29]. Wayne Slater, "Rick Perry says critics of his prayer event are 'intolerant of Christians,'" *Dallas Morning News*, July 14, 2011: http://www.dallasnews.com/news/politics/headlines/20110714-rick-perry-says-critics-of-his-prayer-event-are-intolerant-of-christians.ece

[30]. Zeke Miller, "Rick Perry: Electing Barack Obama Was Our National 'Oops' Moment," BuzzFeed Politics, http://www.buzzfeed.com/zekejmiller/rick-perry-electing-barack-obama-was-our-national

[31]. Arlette Saenz, "Rick Perry's Debate Lapse: 'Oops' - Can't Remember Department of Energy," ABC News, November 9, 2011: http://abcnews.go.com/blogs/politics/2011/11/rick-perrys-debate-lapse-oops-cant-remember-department-of-energy/

[32]. Laura Hoenemeyer, "Face In The News: Rick Perry, Tim Pawlenty, Antonio Villaraigosa," June 25, 2012: http://www.cbsnews.com/8301-3460_162-57459972/face-in-the-news-rick-perry-tim-pawlenty-and-antonio-villaraigosa/

[33]. Chris Wallace, "Rick Perry on Iowa Chances, Mitch McConnell Talks Payroll Tax Extension," December 11, 2011: http://www.foxnews.com/on-air/fox-news-sunday/2011/12/11/rick-perry-iowa-chances-mitch-mcconnell-talks-payroll-tax-cut-extension/print

[34] Press Release, "Statement by Gov. Perry on Supreme Court Ruling Regarding Obamacare," June 28, 2012: http://governor.state.tx.us/news/press-release/17385/

[35]. Press Release, "Statement by Gov. Perry on Congressional Vote to Hold AG Holder in Contempt," June 28, 2012; http://governor.state.tx.us/news/press-release/17387/

[36]. Gromer Jeffers, "Rick Perry blasts President Obama over immigration, disagrees with Texas Republican Party's call for guest worker program," *DallasNews.com* Trailblazer Blog, June 26, 2012: http://trailblazersblog.dallasnews.com/2012/06/rick-perry-blasts-president-obama-over-immigration-disagrees-with-texas-republican-partys-call-for-guest-worker-program.html/

[37] Kevin Drum, "Quote of the Day: How Old is the Earth?," *Mother Jones*, August

18, 2011: http://www.motherjones.com/kevin-drum/2011/08/quote-day-how-old-earth

[38]. Ben Smith, "Perry running to restore military 'respect' for presidency," Ben Smith on Politics and Media blog, *Politico*, August 14, 2011: http://www.politico.com/blogs/bensmith/0811/Perry_running_to_restore_milita ry_respect_for_presidency.html?showall

[39]. Chris Wallace, "Rick Perry on Iowa Chances, Mitch McConnell Talks Payroll Tax Extension," December 11, 2011: http://www.foxnews.com/on-air/fox-news-sunday/2011/12/11/rick-perry-iowa-chances-mitch-mcconnell-talks-payroll-tax-cut-extension/print

[40] Jason Embry, "Perry stops in on Fox News," Statesman.com First Reading blog, November 4, 2010: http://www.statesman.com/blogs/content/shared-gen/blogs/austin/firstreading/entries/2010/11/04/_interesting_tease_on.html

[41]. Press Release. "Gov. Perry: Texas Will Not Expand Medicaid or Implement Health Benefit Exchange," July 9, 2012: http://governor.state.tx.us/news/press-release/17408/

[42]. Jason Embry, 'Perry sits down with Meredith Viera," Statesman.com First Reading blog, November 4, 2010: http://www.statesman.com/blogs/content/shared-gen/blogs/austin/firstreading/entries/2010/11/04/index.html

[43]. Arlette Saenz, "Rick Perry Pulls a George W. Bush," ABC News blog "The Note," June 21, 2011: http://abcnews.go.com/blogs/politics/2011/06/rick-perry-pulls-a-george-w-bush/

[44]. Associated Press, "Some colorful comments by Texas Gov. Rick Perry", Minneapolis *Star Tribune*, August 17, 2011: http://www.startribune.com/politics/national/127897568.html. The video clip of Perry's statement can be found on YouTube: http://www.youtube.com/watch?v=kAXz8NROiaQ

Rick Scott:

[1] UPI, "Governor cuts $600M from Florida budget," UPI.com, May 27, 2011: http://www.upi.com/Top_News/US/2011/05/27/Governor-cuts-600M-from-Florida-budget/UPI-67921306523085/

[2]. Inaugural address, January 4, 2011. http://www.flgov.com/2011/01/04/florida-governor-rick-scott-inaugural-address/

[3]. Jodie Tillman, "Bill requiring welfare recipients to take drug tests headed to governor," *The Miami Herald*, May 5, 2011: http://www.miamiherald.com/2011/05/05/2203328/bill-requiring-welfare-recipients.html#ixzz1UNmvztS1

[4]. Remarks at the University of South Florida, Tampa, January 4, 2011. Bobbie O'Brien, WUSF: "Gov. Scott Defines the Axis of Unemployment,"January 4, 2011: http://www.wusf.usf.edu/news/2011/01/04/gov._scott_defines_the_axis_of_une mployment

[5]. Michelle Hirsch (*The Fiscal Times*), "Meet The Tea Party Governor Everybody Loves To Hate," *Business Insider*, July 20, 2011: http://www.thefiscaltimes.com/Articles/2011/07/20/The-Tea-Party-Governor-

Everybody-Loves-to-Hate.aspx#ixzz1VENUYEOy

[6]. John Kennedy, "Scott not retreating on corp income tax cut," *Palm Beach Post "Post on Politics" blog,* May 2, 2011: http://www.postonpolitics.com/2011/05/scott-not-retreating-on-corp-income-tax-cut/

[7]. Speech at a Tea Party event in Eustis, Florida, February 7, 2011. Tim Padgett, "Rick Scott's Tea-Friendly Budget Cuts: Too Deep?" *Time,* February 14, 2012: http://www.time.com/time/nation/article/0,8599,2049077,00.html

[8]. Interview with Brett M. Decker, *Washington Times.* Brett M. Decker, "Five questions with Gov. Rick Scott," *Washington Times,* February 24, 2012: http://www.washingtontimes.com/news/2012/feb/24/gov-rick-scott-five-questions-with-decker/?utm_source=RSS_Feed&utm_medium=RSS

[9]. Discussing his opposition to the Affordable Care Act. Kevin Sack, "Opposing the health law, Florida refuses millions," *New York Times,* July 31, 2011: http://www.nytimes.com/2011/08/01/us/01florida.html?_r=1&hp

[10]. Speaking at the 2012 Southeastern Press Convention at the Sandestin Golf and Beach Resort in Destin, Florida, July 6, 2012. Jim Turner , "Newspaper Editors Get Big Gulp of Policy Rick Scott-Style," *Sunshine State News,* July 12, 2012: http://www.sunshinestatenews.com/story/newspaper-editors-get-big-gulp-policy-rick-scott-style

[11]. "Scott: Do they call it the Tampa Bay region?," "The Buzz" blog, *Tampa Bay Times,* November 1, 2011: http://www.tampabay.com/blogs/the-buzz-florida-politics/content/scott-do-they-call-it-tampa-bay-region

[12]. Zarzuela Palace, Madrid, Spain, May 22, 2012. Fox News Latino, "Florida Governor Sticks Elephant Foot In Mouth," *Fox News Latino,* May 24, 2012: http://latino.foxnews.com/latino/politics/2012/05/24/florida-governor-sticks-elephant-foot-in-mouth/

[13]. Interview on "The Marc Bernier Show" on WNDB-AM in Daytona Beach cited in *The St. Petersburg Times'* "The Buzz", "Scott: Florida doesn't need more anthropology majors," *TampaBay.com,* October 10, 2011: http://www.tampabay.com/blogs/the-buzz-florida-politics/content/scott-florida-doesnt-need-more-anthropology-majors

[14]. Remarks to a Tallahassee business group on October 10, 2011. Lloyd Dunkelberger, "Scott continues his critique of anthropology degrees," Sarasota *Herald-Tribune,* October 10, 2011: http://htpolitics.com/2011/10/11/scott-continues-his-critique-of-anthropology-degrees/

[15]. Jeremy Wallace, "Scott not so hot on journalism degrees either," Sarasota *Herald-Tribune,* October 14, 2011: http://htpolitics.com/2011/10/14/scott-not-hot-on-journalism-degrees-either/

[16]. Interview with radio station WOKV, Jacksonville, April 17, 2012. Steve Bousquet and Kim Wilmath, "Scott signs $70 billion state budget after $142 million in vetoes," *Miami Herald,* April 17, 2012: http://www.miamiherald.com/2012/04/16/2753732/gov-rick-scott-signs-70-billion.html#storylink=cpy

[17]. Press release, "Gov. Rick Scott reacts to President Obama's claim that America has been "lazy" at attracting businesses," November 14, 2011: http://www.flgov.com/2011/11/14/gov-rick-scott-reacts-to-president-obamas-claim-that-america-has-been-lazy-at-attracting-businesses/

[18]. Tolu Olorunnipa, *Miami Herald* Naked Politics blog, "Scott defends capitalism with 'First they came' Holocaust quote," January 26, 2012: http://miamiherald.typepad.com/nakedpolitics/2012/01/scott-defends-capitalism-with-first-they-came-holocaust-quote.html#storylink=cpy

[19]. Interview with Al Hunt on Bloomberg Television's "Political Capital With Al Hunt", February 2011. Julie Hirschfeld Davis, "Florida's Scott Defends Rejection of Rail Funds as LaHood Cries "Baloney," Bloomberg.com, February 25, 2012: http://www.bloomberg.com/news/2011-02-25/florida-s-scott-defends-refusal-of-high-speed-rail-money-criticizes-obama.html

[20]. July 3, 2012. Jim Turner, "Rick Scott: Obamacare Fight is Just Beginning," *Sunshine State News,* July 3, 2012: http://www.sunshinestatenews.com/story/rick-scott-obamacare-fight-just-beginning

[21]. Press release. Jim Turner, "Rick Scott on Joblessness Drop: More Businesses Opting for Florida Equals More Jobs," *Sunshine State News*, June 15, 2012: http://www.sunshinestatenews.com/story/rick-scott-jobless-drop-more-businesses-opting-florida-equals-more-jobs

[22]. June 25, 2012. Lloyd Dunkelberger, "Rick Scott softens his views on immigration," *Sarasota Herald-Tribune*, June 25, 2012: http://www.heraldtribune.com/article/20120625/ARTICLE/120629732

[23]. "Political Connections" interview with Bay News 9 airing July 2, 2011. Adam C. Smith, "Rick Scott: You bet I want a second term," TampaBay.com, July 2, 2011: http://www.tampabay.com/blogs/the-buzz-florida-politics/content/rick-scott-you-bet-i-want-second-term

[24]. Speaking with southwestern Florida radio stations, June 2012. Jim Turner, "Rick Scott: Wisconsin Validates Florida's Conservative Agenda," *Sunshine State News,* June 9, 2012: http://www.sunshinestatenews.com/story/rick-scott-wisconsin-validates-floridas-conservative-agenda

[25]. Destin, Florida, July, 2010. John Frank, "Open to more drilling - with safeguards - Rick Scott tours the oil-damaged coast,"*St. Petersburg Times,* July 26, 2010: http://www.tampabay.com/news/business/energy/open-to-more-drilling-mdash-with-safeguards-mdash-rick-scott-tours-the/1111250

[26]. Interview with the Sarasota *Herald-Tribune* editorial board, October 10, 2011. Lloyd Dunkelberger, "Scott to push corporate income tax cut," Sarasota *Herald-Tribune*, October 10, 2011: http://htpolitics.com/2011/10/10/scott-to-push-corporate-income-tax-cut/

[27]. Speaking at a July 2011 party at the Governor's Mansion celebrating the signing of anti-abortion bills into law. Matthew Hendley, "Rick Scott Throws an Anti-Abortion Party at the Governor's Mansion," *The Pulp* blog, August 1, 2011: http://blogs.browardpalmbeach.com/pulp/2011/08/rick_scott_anti_abortion_bills_party.php

[28]. Kathleen Haughney, "School prayer bill likely to become law," *Orlando Sentinel*, March 1, 2012: http://www.orlandosentinel.com/news/politics/fl-florida-school-prayer-20120301,0,51857.story

[29]. 2011 State of the State address: http://www.flgov.com/2011/03/08/florida-governor-rick-scott-delivers-state-of-the-state-address/

[30]. Michael Peltier, "Florida governor rejects Republican convention gun ban",
Reuters, May 2, 2012: http://www.reuters.com/article/2012/05/03/us-usa-guns-tampa-idUSBRE8411E320120503

Rick Snyder:
[1]. Chris Christoff and Kathleen Gray, "Rick Snyder Sworn in as Michigan's 48th
Governor," *Detroit Free Press*, January 2, 2011.
www.freep.com/article/20110102/NEWS06/101020560/Rick-Snyder-sworn-in-as-Michigan-s-48th-governor.
[2]. Kathy Barks Hoffman (AP), "Gov. Snyder visits farmer's market on Capitol
lawn," *Deseret News,* August 4, 2011:
https://www.deseretnews.com/article/700168467/Gov-Snyder-visits-farmers-market-on-Capitol-lawn.html
[3]. Karen Bouffard, "'Snyder: Better Transportation, Web Access Key to Finding
Jobs'." *Detroit News,* January 16, 2012:
www.detroitnews.com/article/20120116/POLITICS02/201160398.
[4]. "Michigan's anti-bullying bill becomes law ," *UPI.com*. December 7, 2011:
http://www.upi.com/Top_News/US/2011/12/07/Michigans-anti-bullying-bill-becomes-law/UPI-29731323278874/#ixzz1lkN8Pp8U
[5]. "Michigan drops business tax, hikes others," *UPI.com*. May 13 2011:
http://www.upi.com/Top_News/US/2011/05/13/Michigan-drops-business-tax-hikes-others/UPI-81561305312579/#ixzz1lkOKzpBw.
[6]. Governor's Office, "Pi and Pie Day Proclamation," March 14, 2011,
http://www.michigan.gov/snyder/0,4668,7-277-57577_59874_60073-252647-,00.html
[7]. Melissa Maynard and Jim Malewitz. "Seven questions for Michigan Governor
Rick Snyder," *Stateline* (Pew Center on the States), February 8 2012:
http://www.pewstates.org/projects/stateline/headlines/seven-questions-for-michigan-governor-rick-snyder-85899375421.
[8]. Dave Murray, "Gov. Snyder signs dues collection bill; teachers union leaders
call move 'blatant political retribution,'" *MLive.com*, April 16 2012:
http://www.mlive.com/education/index.ssf/2012/03/gov_snyder_signs_dues_col
lecti.html
[9]. *Detroit Free Press*. "Gov. Rick Snyder to Detroit leaders: Use my absence to
develop a workable response," *Detroit Free Press*, April 16 2012:
http://www.freep.com/article/20120316/NEWS15/203160383/1001/NEWS.
[10]. Leonard Fleming, Darren Nichols, and Karen Bouffard. "Alternate consent
proposal gives Bing more power," *Detroit News*, March 16 2012:
http://www.detroitnews.com/article/20120316/METRO01/203160375/1409/rss
36.
[11]. Rod Meloni, "OK, so now what,?" *ClickonDetroit.com (WDIV-TV)*. March 14,
2012: http://www.clickondetroit.com/money/4yourmoney/OK-so-now-what/-/1719092/9298434/-/cp3w0sz/-/index.html.
[12]. Jonathan Oosting, "There is 'no way in hell' Detroit Mayor Dave Bing will
sign consent agreement as proposed by state," *MLive.com*, March 14, 2012:
http://www.mlive.com/news/detroit/index.ssf/2012/03/detroit_mayor_dave_bin
g_no_way.html.

[13]. Speaking at a town hall meeting on June 8, 2012 at McMorran Main Arena in Port Huron. Jeri Packer, "Snyder touts record, Michigan at Port Huron forum," *The Voice*, June 9, 2012:
http://www.voicenews.com/articles/2012/06/09//news/doc4fd28233c31834540 91535.txt?viewmode=fullstory

[14.] On negotiations for a fiscal plan for Detroit. Suzette Hackney and Paul Egan. "Bing disagrees with governor on control," *Detroit Free Press*, March 14, 2012:
http://www.freep.com/article/20120314/NEWS05/203140462/1001/NEWS

[15]. Remarks at the "Pancakes and Politics" breakfast in Detroit, March 12, 2012. Jonathan Oosting, "Job opportunities key to curbing crime in Detroit," *MLive.com*, March 12, 2012:
http://www.mlive.com/news/detroit/index.ssf/2012/03/gov_rick_snyder_rev_je sse_jack.html

[16]. Remarks in Flint, MI, March 7, 2012 . Kristin Longley, "Gov. Snyder wants to ban property auctions to people with unpaid taxes, blighted property," *MLive.com*, March 12, 2012:
http://www.mlive.com/news/flint/index.ssf/2012/03/gov_snyder_wants_to_ban _proper.html

[17]. Speaking at the West Michigan Asian American Association's annual fundraiser at the Goei Center in Grand Rapids, MI. Nate Reens, "Gov. Snyder on immigration debate: All of us are from different places," *MLive.com*, March 8, 2012:
http://www.mlive.com/news/grand-rapids/index.ssf/2012/03/gov_rick_snyder_on_immigration.html

[18]. Kristin Longley, "Gov. Snyder unveils public safety proposal in Flint calling for more state police, forensic techs in high-crime cities," *MLive.com*, March 7, 2012:
http://www.mlive.com/news/flint/index.ssf/2012/03/gov_snyder_unveils_public _safe.html

[19]. Speaking at unveiling of crime plan in Flint, March 7, 2012. Associated Press, "Snyder unveils police plan; State troopers would fight crime in cities," *The Morning Sun*, March 8, 2012:
http://www.themorningsun.com/articles/2012/03/08/news/srv0000023853522.t xt?viewmode=default

[20]. Erica Perdue, "Gov. Snyder elaborates on public safety plan, 'trying to change the whole culture,'"*MLive.com*, March 8, 2012:
http://www.mlive.com/news/saginaw/index.ssf/2012/03/gov_snyder_elaborates _on_publi.html

[21]. Budget address, February 2012. Associated Press, "Snyder has wide-ranging plan to improve public safety," *The Morning Sun*, March 6, 2012.

[22]. Interview with Glenn Gilbert. Glenn Gilbert, "Opinion: Michigan is now a good economic example to the nation," *The Oakland Press*, March 2, 2012.

[23]. Speaking at a victory celebration for Mitt Romney after the Michigan primary in Novi, Michigan, Feb. 28, 2012. Melissa Anders, "Michigan primary: Romney dodges bullet by winning here," *MLive.com*, February 28, 2012:
http://www.mlive.com/politics/index.ssf/2012/02/michigan_primary_romney_d odges.html?utm_source=feedburner&utm_medium=feed&utm_campaign=Feed% 3A+michigan-elections+%28Michigan+Elections+News%29

[24]. Thomas Fitzgerald, "Anti-bailout stance could hurt GOP in Michigan," *The Big Tent* blog (*Philadelphia Inquirer*), February 28, 2012:
http://www.philly.com/philly/blogs/big_tent/Anti-bailout-stance-could-hurt-GOP-in-Mich.html

[25]. Jack Spencer, "Snyder Signs Bill Reinforcing That Graduate Students are Students, Not Employees," *CAPCON* blog, Mackinac Center for Public Policy, March 24, 2012: http://www.mackinac.org/16596

[26]. Speaking while in Europe on a trade mission. Paul Egan, "Snyder asks unions to ease up on right to work efforts, too," *Lansing State Journal*, March 20, 2012:
http://www.lansingstatejournal.com/article/20120320/NEWS04/303200035/Snyder-asks-unions-ease-up-right-work-efforts-too

[27]. Testifying before a congressional committee, Washington, DC. Henry C. Jackson, "Rick Snyder Says His Approach Differs from Other Midwestern Governors,"*Huffington Post*, January 12, 2012:
http://www.huffingtonpost.com/2012/02/02/rick-snyder-says-hes-diff_n_1249439.html

[28]. Zoe Clark, "Snyder signs partial birth abortion law," Michigan Radio, October 12, 2011: http://michiganradio.org/post/snyder-signs-partial-birth-abortion-law

[29]. Speaking in Port Huron, Michigan. Holly Setter, "Gov. Rick Snyder draws a crowd," *thetimesherald.com*, June 8, 2012:
http://www.thetimesherald.com/article/BP/20120609/NEWS05/306090002/Gov-Rick-Snyder-draws-crowd?odyssey=nav | head

[30]. Interview by Charlie Langton for WXYT-AM Radio (News Talk 1270) at Mackinac Policy Conference, Mackinac Island, May 31, 2012. Charlie Langton, "The Relentless Positivity of Gov. Rick Snyder," CBS Detroit, May 312, 2012:
http://detroit.cbslocal.com/2012/05/31/the-relentless-positivity-of-gov-rick-snyder/

[31]. Keynote address at the Detroit Regional Chamber's Mackinac Policy Conference, Mackinac Island, Michigan. Matt Roush, "Snyder on Mackinac: Hire Veterans, Brag About Michigan," WWJ Radio/CBS Detroit, May 29, 2012:
http://detroit.cbslocal.com/2012/05/29/snyder-on-mackinac-hire-veterans-brag-about-michigan/

[32]. Speaking at a town hall meeting at the La-Z-Boy Center at Monroe County Community College, Monroe, Michigan, June 25, 2012. Charles Slat, "Gov. Snyder holds town hall at MCCC," *Monroe News*, June 26, 2012:
http://www.monroenews.com/news/2012/jun/25/gov-snyder-holds-town-hall-mccc/

[33]. 2011 Inaugural Address, January 2011. Natalie Gonnella, "Quote of the day: Governor Rick Snyder calls for sacrifice and ingenuity to move Michigan forward," *Conservative Home*, January 2, 2011:
http://conhomeusa.typepad.com/bigideas/2011/01/asas.html

[34]. Keynote address at the Detroit Regional Chamber's Mackinac Policy Conference, Mackinac Island, Michigan. Paul Egan, "Michigan Gov. Rick Snyder is working on strategies for when the good economic times return to state," *Detroit Free Press*, June 1, 2012:
http://www.freep.com/article/20120601/NEWS15/206010394/1001/rss01

[35]. More remarks from Mackinac Policy Conference speech. John Flesher (AP),

"Michigan needs long-term financial plans," *Yahoo! News,* May 31, 2012:
http://news.yahoo.com/snyder-michigan-needs-long-term-financial-plans-
192915897-finance.html;_ylt=A2KJ3CcAT9NPKlgA7eLQtDMD
[36]. "Gov. Rick Snyder: 'I'm Encouraged By Romney's Education Reform Plan,'"
May 23, 2012. Mitt Romney presidential campaign website:
http://www.mittromney.com/news/press/2012/05/gov-rick-snyder-im-
encouraged-romneys-education-reform-plan
[37]. Facebook post, Rick Snyder for Michigan, June 5, 2012:
https://www.facebook.com/RickForMichigan
[38] Facebook post, Rick Snyder for Michigan, June 5, 2012:
https://www.facebook.com/RickForMichigan
[39]. Facebook post, Rick Snyder for Michigan, May 24, 2012:
https://www.facebook.com/photo.php?fbid=10150840905268359&set=a.102695
878358.93439.93955318358&type=1&theater
[40]. Governor's Blog, "Why We Must Act Now on Healthcare," July 3, 2012.
Posted on Rick Snyder for Michigan Facebook page:
https://www.facebook.com/notes/rick-snyder-for-michigan/governors-blog-why-
we-must-act-now-on-health-care/10150926248928359
[41]. Facebook post, Rick Snyder for Michigan, February 16, 2012:
https://www.facebook.com/RickForMichigan/posts/10150559724528359
[42]. Remarks at Bethel East Baptist Church, Detroit, June 26, 2012. Jonathan
Oosting, "Lost in shouting, Snyder shares vision for Detroit: Making things 'less
worse' isn't good enough," *MLive.com,* June 27, 2012:
http://www.mlive.com/news/detroit/index.ssf/2012/06/lost_in_shouting_sndyer
_shares.html
[43]. Speaking to a group of new Chrysler employees, Auburn HIlls, Michigan, May
14, 2012. Michael Wayland, "Snyder: Immigrants, native Michiganders can help
state lead nation in talent," *MLive.com,* May 15, 2012:
http://www.mlive.com/news/detroit/index.ssf/2012/05/snyder_immigrants_nati
ve_michi.html
[44]. Speaking at a town hall meeting on June 8, 2012 at McMorran Main Arena in
Port Huron. Jeri Packer, "Snyder touts record, Michigan at Port Huron forum,"
The Voice, June 9, 2012:
http://www.voicenews.com/articles/2012/06/09//news/doc4fd28233c31834540
91535.txt?viewmode=fullstory

Scott Walker
[1]. Patrick Marley and Rick Bergquist, "Walker wins governor's race on promise of
jobs," *Milwaukee Journal Sentinel,* November 3, 2010:
http://www.jsonline.com/news/statepolitics/106580158.html
[2]. Ben Smith, " Wisconsin Gov on IL tax vote: 'Escape to Wisconsin,'" *Politico,*
January 12, 2011:
http://www.politico.com/blogs/bensmith/0111/Wisconsin_Gov_on_IL_tax_vot
e_Escape_to_Wisconsin.html?showall
[3]. "Transcript of prank Koch-Walker conversation," *Wisconsin State Journal,*
February 23, 2011: http://host.madison.com/wsj/article_531276b6-3f6a-11e0-
b288-001cc4c002e0.html

[4]. Peter Hamby, "Walker: 'I was the original Tea Party in Wisconsin," *CNN Political Ticker*, Sept. 27, 2010.
CNNhttp://politicalticker.blogs.cnn.com/2010/09/27/walker-i-was-the-original-tea-party-in-wisconsin/

[5]. Meredith Shiner, "Wisconsin Gov. Scott Walker: No compromise on union rights," *Politico*, February 21, 2011:
http://www.politico.com/news/stories/0211/49919.html#ixzz1VEJf0WSS

[6]. Jason Stein: "Better late than never: Quinn makes good on bet," *Milwaukee Journal Sentinel*, Augusts 2, 2011:
http://www.jsonline.com/news/statepolitics/126594688.html

[7]. Tim Jones, "Walker Union Fight Intensifies as Wisconsin's Recalls Threaten Republicans," *Bloomberg News*, August 8, 2011:
http://www.bloomberg.com/news/2011-08-08/walker-union-fight-intensifies-as-wisconsin-s-recalls-threaten-republicans.html

[8]. Mary Spicuzza, "Both parties still hold hope for Wisconsin recalls," *Green Bay Press-Gazette*, August 14, 2011:
http://www.greenbaypressgazette.com/article/20110814/GPG0101/108140590&located=rss

[9]. Gov. Walker appearing on MSNBC's "Morning Joe," August 12, 2011: Paige Lavender, "Scott Walker Reacts to Wisconsin Recall Election Results," *The Huffington Post*, August 12, 2011:
http://www.huffingtonpost.com/2011/08/12/scott-walker-wisconsin-recall-election_n_925331.html

[10]. Timothy Jones, *Bloomberg BusinessWeek*, August 11, 2011:
http://www.businessweek.com/news/2011-08-11/walker-says-wisconsin-voters-have-had-it-with-recalls.html

[11]. Timothy Jones, *Bloomberg BusinessWeek*, August 11, 2011:
http://www.businessweek.com/news/2011-08-11/walker-says-wisconsin-voters-have-had-it-with-recalls.html

[12]. Patrick Marley, "Walker says he wants to work with both sides," *Milwaukee Journal Sentinel*, August 10, 2011:
http://www.jsonline.com/blogs/news/127437528.html?sort=last+to+first

[13]. Kevin Fischer, "Quotes from Scott Walker's victory speech," *FranklinNow.com,* September 14, 2010:
http://www.franklinnow.com/blogs/communityblogs/102925864.html

[14]. "A collection of quotes from Gov. Walker's congressional testimony," *Dane101.com*, April 14, 2011:
http://dane101.com/current/2011/04/14/a_collection_of_quotes_from_gov_walkers_congressional_testimony

[15]. Interview with Reuters at the National Governors' Association meeting in Salt Lake City. Edith Honan (Reuters), "Scott Walker Concedes Mistakes, Defends Policies," *The Huffington Post*, July 16, 2011:
http://www.huffingtonpost.com/2011/07/16/scott-walker-mistakes-policies_n_900820.html

[16]. Radio interview with Charlie Sykes, March 12, 2012. Chris Bowers, "Scott Walker, $144,423 annual salary, says he could 'make some real money' in the private sector," *Daily Kos*, March 13, 2012:

http://www.dailykos.com/story/2012/03/13/1074112/-Scott-Walker-144-423-annual-salary-says-he-could-make-some-real-money-in-the-private-sector

[17]. Interviewed by George Stephanopoulos on ABC's "Good Morning America," February 21, 2011. Mark Joyella, "Wisconsin Governor Scott Walker Denies Union Busting on *GMA*," *Mediaite* blog, February 21, 2011. http://www.mediaite.com/tv/wisconsin-governor-scott-walker-denies-union-busting-on-gma/

[18]. Interview with Rick Brody of CBN, Executive Mansion, Maple Bluff, Wisconsin, April 1, 2012. David Brody, "Exclusive: Scott Walker on Recall: 'God's Got A Plan,'" CBN.com, April 3, 2012: http://blogs.cbn.com/thebrodyfile/archive/2012/04/04/exclusive-scott-walker-on-recall-gods-got-a-plan.aspx

[19]. Carol Joffe, "It's Not Just Unions: Scott Walker is Busting Planned Parenthood, Too," *Beacon Broadside* blog, March 8, 2011: http://www.beaconbroadside.com/broadside/2011/03/its-not-just-unions.html

[20]. Hannah O'Brien, "Wisconsin Governor Scott Walker says new laws protect families," *Appleton Post-Crescent*, April 13, 2012: http://www.postcrescent.com/article/20120413/APC010405/204130489/Wisconsin-Governor-Scott-Walker-says-new-laws-protect-families

[21]. Scott Bauer, "Wisconsin Governor Scott Walker signs Voter ID law," *Appleton Post-Crescent*, May 26, 2011.

[22]. Jim Salter (AP), "Walker tells NRA crowd that recall issue extends beyond Wisconsin," *Wisconsin State Journal*, April 13, 2012: http://host.madison.com/wsj/news/local/govt-and-politics/walker-tells-nra-crowd-that-recall-issue-extends-beyond-wisconsin/article_fb74379e-85bf-11e1-bf55-0019bb2963f4.html

[23]. Amanda Terkel, "Scott Walker Defends Equal Pay Law Repeal: 'Lawyers Could Clog Up The Legal System,'" *Huffington Post*, April 18, 2012: http://www.huffingtonpost.com/2012/04/18/scott-walker-equal-pay-repeal_n_1434886.html?1334784763

[24]. David A. Patten and Kathleen Walter, "Scott Walker: States Headed the Way of Greece Without Reforms," *Newsmax*, April 22, 2012: http://www.newsmax.com/Newsfront/walker-greece-state-unions/2012/04/22/id/436678

[25]. David A. Patten and Kathleen Walter, "Scott Walker to Newsmax: Obama's Machine Spending $60 Million to Defeat Me," *Newsmax*, April 22, 2012: http://www.newsmax.com/Headline/walker-wisconsin-recall-unions/2012/04/22/id/436674

[26]. David A. Patten and Kathleen Walter, "Gov. Walker Predicts: We Will Beat Big Labor's Recall," *Newsmax*, April 22, 2012: http://www.newsmax.com/Headline/walker-wisconsin-recall-unions/2012/04/22/id/436674

[27]. David A. Patten and Kathleen Walter, "Wisconsin's Walker: Jobs Will Surge Once I Prevail," *Newsmax*, April 22, 2012: http://www.newsmax.com/US/walker-job-creation-wisconsin/2012/04/22/id/436675

[28]. Bill Glauber and Steve Schultze, "Walker stands by bargaining bill, jobs promise," *Milwaukee Journal Sentinel*, May 2, 2012:

http://www.jsonline.com/news/statepolitics/walker-stands-by-bargaining-bill-even-if-hes-recalled-sf58so3-149925925.html

[29]. Eric Kleefeld, "Walker to Christian Right Supporters - Pray For Me And Help Out The Campaign," *Talking Points Memo*, May 2, 2012: http://2012.talkingpointsmemo.com/2012/05/walker-to-christian-right-supporters-pray-for-me-and-help-out-the-campaign.php?ref=fpb

[30]. Jason Stein and Patrick Marley, "In film, Walker talks of 'divide and conquer' union strategy," *Milwaukee Journal Sentinel*, May 10, 2012: http://www.jsonline.com/news/statepolitics/in-film-walker-talks-of-divide-and-conquer-strategy-with-unions-8o57h6f-151049555.html

[31]. Kate Golden and Amy Karon, "Preaching to the choir: Conservative media and friendly audiences are Walker PR linchpins," *The Capital Times*, May 16, 2012: http://host.madison.com/ct/news/local/govt-and-politics/preaching-to-the-choir-conservative-media-and-friendly-audiences-are/article_5f3473fc-9ecf-11e1-bdfc-001a4bcf887a.html

[32]. Scott Bauer, "Walker says he's not afraid to lose recall," *Wisconsin State Journal*, May 18, 2012: http://host.madison.com/wsj/news/local/govt-and-politics/elections/walker-says-he-s-not-afraid-to-lose-recall/article_c883cb08-a066-11e1-8866-0019bb2963f4.html

[33]. CBS News, "Walker: Voters want tough decisions to be made,"CBS Evening News, June 6, 2012: http://www.cbsnews.com/8301-18563_162-57448652/walker-voters-want-tough-decisions-to-be-made/

[34]. Bill Glauber, "Walkers relax as political whirlwind settles," *Milwaukee Journal Sentinel*, June 9, 2012: http://www.jsonline.com/news/statepolitics/walkers-relax-as-political-whirlwind-settles-mc5n7da-158317135.html

[35]. James Hohmann, "Scott Walker wants national role," *Politico*, June 26, 2012: http://www.politico.com/news/stories/0612/77851.html

ABOUT THE AUTHORS

Amy Fried is Professor of Political Science at the University of Maine. She is the author of two scholarly books, *Muffled Echoes* (Columbia University Press) and *Pathways to Polling* (Routledge), as well as numerous peer-reviewed articles and book chapters. Fried writes a biweekly column at the *Bangor Daily News*, blogs at Pollways.com and tweets as @ASFried. She lives in Bangor, Maine with her husband and son.

Jim Melcher is Associate Professor of Political Science at the University of Maine at Farmington, where he has taught since 1999. He is frequently interviewed about American politics by media outlets both inside and outside of Maine, has won six teaching awards during his career and has authored many scholarly articles and papers. He and his wife Nancy Finnegan live in Augusta, Maine.

www.ingramcontent.com/pod-product-compliance
Lightning Source LLC
Chambersburg PA
CBHW020434290526
45785CB00002B/840